Nick Grosso

# Ingredient X

T0258369

Methuen Drama

Published by Methuen Drama 2010

1 3 5 7 9 10 8 6 4 2

Methuen Drama
A & C Black Publishers Limited
36 Soho Square
London W1D 3QY
www.methuendrama.com

ISBN 978 1 408 13215 9

A CIP catalogue record for this book is available from
the British Library

Typeset by MPS Limited, a Macmillan Company

# ROYAL COURT

The Royal Court Theatre presents

# INGREDIENT X

## by **Nick Grosso**

First performance at The Royal Court Jerwood Theatre Upstairs, Sloane Square, London on Thursday 20 May 2010.

# INGREDIENT X

by Nick Grosso

*in order of appearance*
Frank **James Lance**
Rosanna **Lesley Sharp**
Deanne **Lisa Palfrey**
Katie **Indira Varma**

Director **Deborah Bruce**
Designer **Ben Stones**
Lighting **Matt Drury**
Sound **David McSeveney**
Casting Director **Julia Horan**
Production Manager **Tariq Rifaat**
Dialect Coach **Jan Haydn Rowles**
Stage Managers **Susie Jenkins, Erin Murphy**
Stage Management Work Placement **Harriet Stewart**
Costume Supervisor **Iona Kenrick**

**With thanks to Anne Skorzewski on placement from Kingston University for her assistance with the production.**

**Additional thanks to Peter Jones of Sloane Square for their generous contribution towards the set dressing.**

Stage Management also wish to thank Brompton Bikes for their help with this production.

## NICK GROSSO (Writer)

FOR THE ROYAL COURT: Kosher Harry, Real Classy Affair (at Ambassadors), Sweetheart, Peaches (with National), Mama Don't (for the Young People's Theatre).

## DEBORAH BRUCE (Director)

FOR THE ROYAL COURT: Scarborough (& Edinburgh Festival Fringe with Northern Firebrand), Made of Stone.

OTHER THEATRE INCLUDES: Helen (Shakespeare's Globe); Geoff Dead:Disco For Sale (Live Theatre, Newcastle); Blame (Arcola/Tour); My Own Show (Stephen Joseph Theatre); The Unexpected Man, In Praise of Love (Theatre Royal, Bath); Musik (Oxford Stage Co.); Taking Sides (No.1 Tour); Death and the Ploughman (Gate, Notting Hill); Mrs Warren's Profession (Bristol Old Vic); Behsharam (Soho/Birmingham Rep.); The Woman Who Swallowed a Pin (Southwark Playhouse); Making Noise Quietly (Oxford Stage Co./Whitehall Theatre/Tour); The Asylum Project (Riverside); The Inheritor (NT Studio); Romeo and Juliet (Chester Gateway); The Glass Menagerie, Our Country's Good, My Sister in this House, Hello and Goodbye, Oleanna (Theatr Clwyd).

## MATT DRURY (Lighting)

FOR THE ROYAL COURT: The Author, Wall, Seven Jewish Children, Over There, The Stone, Shades, Birth of a Nation, The Mother.

OTHER THEATRE INCLUDES: Tin Horizon (Theatre 503); Private Lives, Same Time Next Year, Absent Friends, Absurd Person Singular, Deadly Nightcap, Bedroom Farce, Sweet Revenge, Joking Apart, Dead Certain, Cinderella, Dangerous Obsession, Spider's Web (Theatre Royal Windsor); Under Their Hats (Thorndike Theatre, Leatherhead & West End), Nicholas Nickleby, The Hollow Crown, Guys & Dolls, (Thorndike Theatre, Leatherhead); The Flipside, Shirley Valentine, The Gentle Hook (Bill Kenwright); Fools Rush In (UK Tour); Funny Money (UK Tour); Two of A Kind (UK Tour); Catch Me if You Can (UK Tour); Framed (National); Cassie (Everyman, Cheltenham); Scooping the Pot (UK Tour); Daemons (European Tour); The Hollow (UK Tour), The Unexpected Guest (UK Tour); The Haunted Hotel (UK Tour); Arsenic & Old Lace (UK Tour); An Ideal Husband (UK Tour).

Matt is Head of Lighting at the Royal Court.

## JAMES LANCE (Frank)

THEATRE INCLUDES: Pythonesque (Edinburgh Festival Fringe); Ordinary Dreams (Trafalgar Studios); Pirandello's Henry IV (Donmar); Christmas, A Place at the Table, The Back Room (Bush); Tape (New Venture Theatre); The Inland Sea (Wilton's Music Hall); Penny for a Song (Whitehall Theatre); Queen Christina (Labyrinth); Elegies for Angels and Raging Queens (Kings Head); Brilliant The Dinosaur (Chichester, RFH).

TELEVISION INCLUDES: Moving Wallpaper, Marple, Boy Meets Girl, No Heroics, Biffovision, Hotel Babylon, The Last Enemy, Sensitive Skin, And Now The Weather, Losing It, The Impressionists, Saxondale, Sensitive Skin, Absolute Power, Top Buzzer, Teachers, Rescue Me, The Book Group, Always Be Close, People Like Us, Spaced, Smack The Pony, The Marchioness, Then, Bruiser, I'm Alan Partridge, Waiting for God, Absolutely Fabulous, Conjugal Rites, Teenage Health Freak, The Upper Hand, Second Thoughts, Family Money.

FILM INCLUDES: Bel Ami, Bronson, City Rats, Rubbish, Mr Right, Marie Antoinette, Hard to Swallow, The Lead, Call Register, Late Night Shopping, It's Not You It's Me, Subterrain, The Search for John Gissing, Once Again, Fistful of Fingers.

## DAVID McSEVENEY (Sound)

FOR THE ROYAL COURT: Posh, Disconnect, Cock, Seven Jewish Children, A Miracle, Shades, The Stone, The Girlfriend Experience (&Theatre Royal Plymouth & Young Vic), Contractions, Fear & Misery/War & Peace.

OTHER THEATRE INCLUDES: Tin Horizon (Theatre 503); Gaslight (Old Vic); Charley's Aunt, An Hour and a Half Late (Theatre Royal Bath); A Passage to India, After Mrs Rochester, Madame Bovary (Shared Experience); Men Should Weep, Rookery Nook (Oxford Stage Company); Othello (Southwark Playhouse).

AS ASSISTANT DESIGNER: The Permanent Way (Out of Joint); My Brilliant Divorce, Auntie and Me (West End); Accidental Death of an Anarchist (Donmar).

ORIGINAL MUSIC: The BFG (Secret Theatre Productions).

David is Head of Sound at the Royal Court.

## LISA PALFREY (Deanne)

FOR THE ROYAL COURT: Under the Blue Sky.

OTHER THEATRE INCLUDES: Small Change, Ghosts (Sherman Theatre Company); Blink(Tour/Off Broadway); Gathered Dust & Dead Skin (Live); Festen (Almeida/West End); The Iceman Cometh (Almeida); Cardiff East, Under Milkwood (National); House of America, Flowers of the Dead Sea (UK Tour).

TELEVISION INCLUDES: Pen Talar, Blodau, Pobol y Cwm, The Inspector Lynley Mysteries, If Wishes Were Horses, The Bill, Outside The Rules, Casualty, Green Eyed Monster, Split Second, Magistrates, Mind Games, Lord Of Misrule, Soldier, Soldier.

FILM INCLUDES: Guest House Paradiso, House of America, The Deadness of Dad, The Englishman Who Went Up a Hill But Came Down a Mountain, Maybe Baby.

## LESLEY SHARP (Rosanna)

FOR THE ROYAL COURT: Top Girls, Our Country's Good/The Recruiting Officer, Greenland, Road, Shirley, Gone, Who Knew Mackenzie?

OTHER THEATRE INCLUDES: Ghosts (Duchess Theatre, West End); Little Voice (Vaudeville, West End); Harper Regan, Mother Courage, Uncle Vanya, Murmuring Judges, Six Characters in Search of an Author, Fathers & Sons, Ting Tang Mine, True Dare Kiss, Command or Promise (National); God of Hell (Donmar); Playing with Trains, Mary & Lizzie, Cyrano De Bergerac, King Lear, Maydays, The Body, Macbeth (RSC); Caverns of Dreams, Hindle Wakes (Liverpool Playhouse); Green, Face Value (Contact Theatre, Manchester).

TELEVISION INCLUDES: Cranford, Poirot, Moving On, The Diary of Ann Frank, Red Riding, Doctor Who, The Children, Afterlife, Planespotting, The Survivors, Carla, Carrie's War, The Second Coming, Bob & Rose, Clocking Off, Nature Boy, Daylight Robbery, Great Expectations, Playing the Field, Moonstone, Common as Muck, Prime Suspect, Dandelion Dead, Frank Stubbs, Road, Top Girls, Wedded, Tartuffe, Night Voice, Debt.

FILM INCLUDES: Inkheart, Vera Drake, Cheeky, From Hell, The Full Monty, Naked, Priest, Close My Eyes, The Rachel Papers, Rita, Sue & Bob Too.

AWARDS INCLUDE: Golden Nymph Best Actress Award for Bob & Rose and Afterlife, Press Guild Best Actress Award for Clocking Off and Bob & Rose, RTS Northwest Best Actress Award for Bob & Rose, Time Out Best New Actress Award for Road.

## BEN STONES (Designer)

THEATRE INCLUDES: Creditors, Kiss Of The Spider Woman (Donmar); Beautiful Thing (Sound Theatre, West End); Humble Boy, Paradise Lost, Someone Who'll Watch Over Me, Just Between Ourselves (Theatre Royal Northampton); Paradise Lost (Headlong Theatre); The Arab Israeli Cookbook (Tricycle); The Mighty Boosh, Mitchell and Webb Live! (Phil McIntyre UK Tour); The Vegemite Tales (The Venue, Leicester Square); When Five Years Pass (Arcola); The Herbal Bed, The Real Thing (Salisbury Playhouse); Taste of Honey, Salt (Royal Exchange Manchester); Romeo & Juliet (Shakespeare's Globe); My Mother Said I Never Should (Watford Palace Theatre); My Dad's a Birdman, An Enemy of the People (Sheffield Crucible); Speaking in Tongues (Duke of York's, West End).

AWARDS INCLUDE: 2003 Linbury Prize Commision.

## INDIRA VARMA (Katie)

FOR THE ROYAL COURT: The Vertical Hour, The Country.

OTHER THEATRE INCLUDES: Twelfth Night, The Vortex, Privates on Parade (Donmar); The Skin of Our Teeth (Young Vic); Five Gold Rings (Almeida); Celebration (Almeida/Broadway); Ivanov, Remembrance of Things Past, Othello (National); Three Sisters (Oxford Stage Company); As You Like It (Nottingham Playhouse); One for the Road (New Ambassadors/Broadway).

TELEVISION INCLUDES: Luther, Hustle, Inside the Box, Moses Jones, Bones, Whistleblowers, 3lbs, Torchwood, Inspector Lynley Mysteries, Waste of Shame, Broken News, Love Soup, Quartermass, Rome, Donovan, Reversals, The Sea Captain's Tale, Attachments, The Whistleblower, Other People's Children, In a Land of Plenty, Ten Crazy Days, Psychos.

FILM INCLUDES: Risk Addiction, Bride & Prejudice, Jinnah, Sixth Happiness, Clancy's Kitchen, Phoenix, Kama Sutra

**Jerwood Theatre Upstairs**

14 July – 14 August

# spur of the moment
## by anya reiss

"I was always in such a rush to grow up I never thought about what I'd do when I got there."

Pre-teen Delilah enjoys High School Musical, swim parties and ogling the lodger. Whilst her parents throw verbal grenades at one another, they barely notice their 21 year old tenant starting to notice her.

Supported by
the Jerwood Charitable Foundation

### JERWOOD
NEW PLAYWRIGHTS

**020 7565 5000** Tickets £15 (Mondays all seats £10)
**www.royalcourttheatre.com**
Royal Court Theatre, Sloane Square, London, SW1W 8AS

# THE ENGLISH STAGE COMPANY
# AT THE ROYAL COURT THEATRE

*'For me the theatre is really a religion or way of life. You must decide what you feel the world is about and what you want to say about it, so that everything in the theatre you work in is saying the same thing ... A theatre must have a recognisable attitude. It will have one, whether you like it or not.'*

George Devine, first artistic director of the English Stage Company: notes for an unwritten book.

photo: Stephen Cummiskey

As Britain's leading national company dedicated to new work, the Royal Court Theatre produces new plays of the highest quality, working with writers from all backgrounds, and addressing the problems and possibilities of our time.

"The Royal Court has been at the centre of British cultural life for the past 50 years, an engine room for new writing and constantly transforming the theatrical culture." Stephen Daldry

Since its foundation in 1956, the Royal Court has presented premieres by almost every leading contemporary British playwright, from John Osborne's Look Back in Anger to Caryl Churchill's A Number and Tom Stoppard's Rock 'n' Roll. Just some of the other writers to have chosen the Royal Court to premiere their work include Edward Albee, John Arden, Richard Bean, Samuel Beckett, Edward Bond, Leo Butler, Jez Butterworth, Martin Crimp, Ariel Dorfman, Stella Feehily, Christopher Hampton, David Hare, Eugène Ionesco, Ann Jellicoe, Terry Johnson, Sarah Kane, David Mamet, Martin McDonagh, Conor McPherson, Joe Penhall, Lucy Prebble, Mark Ravenhill, Simon Stephens, Wole Soyinka, Polly Stenham, David Storey, Debbie Tucker Green, Arnold Wesker and Roy Williams.

"It is risky to miss a production there." Financial Times

In addition to its full-scale productions, the Royal Court also facilitates international work at a grass roots level, developing exchanges which bring young writers to Britain and sending British writers, actors and directors to work with artists around the world. The research and play development arm of the Royal Court Theatre, The Studio, finds the most exciting and diverse range of new voices in the UK. The Studio runs play-writing groups including the Young Writers Programme, Critical Mass for black, Asian and minority ethnic writers and the biennial Young Writers Festival. For further information, go to www.royalcourttheatre.com/ywp.

"Yes, the Royal Court is on a roll. Yes, Dominic Cooke has just the genius and kick that this venue needs... It's fist-bitingly exciting." Independent

Supported by
**ARTS COUNCIL ENGLAND**

# PROGRAMME SUPPORTERS

The Royal Court (English Stage Company Ltd) receives its principal funding from Arts Council England, London. It is also supported financially by a wide range of private companies, charitable and public bodies, and earns the remainder of its income from the box office and its own trading activities.

The Genesis Foundation supports the Royal Court's work with International Playwrights. Theatre Local is sponsored by Bloomberg. The Jerwood Charitable Foundation supports new plays by new playwrights through the Jerwood New Playwrights series.

The Artistic Director's Chair is supported by a lead grant from The Peter Jay Sharp Foundation, contributing to the activities of the Artistic Director's office. Over the past ten years the BBC has supported the Gerald Chapman Fund for directors.

# FOR THE ROYAL COURT

Royal Court Theatre, Sloane Square, London SW1W 8AS
Tel: 020 7565 5050 Fax: 020 7565 5001
info@royalcourttheatre.com, www.royalcourttheatre.com

**Characters**

**Deanne**
**Frank**
**Katie**
**Rosanna**

*The playtext that follows was correct at time of going to press, but night have changed during rehearsal.*

## Part One

*Frank is on the sofa watching telly. Late thirties. The entry phone goes. He gets up and buzzes downstairs open then opens the front door to the open-plan flat. He sits back down on the sofa. Rosanna and Deanne walk on through the front door. Both mid-forties.*

**Rosanna**  Who's winning?

**Frank**  Nil-nil.

**Rosanna**  Come on Italy.

**Deanne**  Who's playing?

**Rosanna**  Italy.

**Rosanna** *cracks up.*

**Deanne**  Italy and who?

**Frank**  Scotland.

**Rosanna**  Don't you know anything?

**Deanne**  I know how to give you a slap.

**Rosanna**  Oh yeah?

**Deanne**  Yeah.

**Rosanna** *and* **Deanne** *crack up.*

What's so important about this game then?

**Rosanna**  Tell her Frank.

**Frank**  Crunch game.

**Deanne**  Really?

**Rosanna**  Scotland win Italy are out tell her Frank.

**Deanne**  Is it?

**Frank**  It is.

**Deanne**  Are Scotland good?

**Frank** *and* **Rosanna** *look nonplussed.*

Are they?

**Rosanna**   Is that what you just asked?

**Frank**   No they're not.

**Deanne**   So what's the problem?

**Rosanna**   Is there a problem? Did someone say there was a problem? I didn't hear anyone say there was a problem. Scotland need to win they won't win Italy will knock them out Italy will go through. That's about the gist.

**Frank**   Oh shit.

**Deanne**   What?

**Frank**   Scotland just scored.

**Rosanna**   What?

**Frank**   Offside. Thank fuck for that.

**Rosanna**   Come on Italy get your fucking *act* together.

**Frank**   I swear to god we're playing shit.

**Rosanna**   How long left?

**Frank**   Minutes.

**Rosanna**   Blow your whistle ref.

**Frank**   Fucking ref doesn't know what day it is.

**Deanne**   That wasn't offside.

**Rosanna**   Shut up you.

**Deanne**   Was it though?

**Rosanna**   What would *you* know?

**Frank**   No it wasn't.

**Deanne**   It wasn't.

**Frank**   It wasn't.

**Rosanna**   Bout time that ref gave us something.

**Deanne**    Have you been watching?

**Rosanna**    No.

**Deanne**    Well then.

**Frank**    Referee's a cunt.

**Rosanna**    You see.

**Frank**    Hates Italians.

**Rosanna**    They *all* do.

**Frank**    It's cos we won the World Cup.

**Rosanna**    They can't handle it.

**Frank**    It's because whenever their wives see us they want to fuck us.

**Rosanna**    Is that right?

**Frank**    Don't shoot the messenger.

**Rosanna**    Blow your fucking whistle.

**Frank**    Fucking tit. Just cos your wife wants to fuck me.

**Deanne**    He just denied them a goal.

**Rosanna**    It wasn't a goal.

**Deanne**    It was.

**Rosanna**    What would *you* know?

**Deanne**    Frank was it a goal?

**Frank**    It was a goal.

**Deanne**    You see. You've bribed him. Same old Italy. Always cheating.

**Frank**    Do you mind?

**Deanne**    Good-looking though.

**Rosanna**    Where's Katie?

**Frank**   Feeding Bubba.

**Rosanna**   Can I go through?

**Frank**   She's probably putting him to bed.

**Deanne**   Yeah.

**Frank**   She'll be out in a minute.

**Rosanna**   Go on then.

**Frank**   What?

**Rosanna**   Pour us a drink.

**Deanne**   Get the drinks.

**Frank** *gets up.*

**Frank**   What do you want?

**Rosanna**   I don't know, what have you got?

**Deanne**   What have you got?

**Frank**   I don't know.

**Deanne**   Gin.

**Rosanna**   Vodka.

**Deanne**   I like vodka.

**Rosanna**   I like gin.

**Rosanna** *and* **Deanne** *crack up.*

**Frank**   Vodka and gin it is.

**Rosanna**   Not too much vodka in my gin.

**Rosanna** *and* **Deanne** *crack up.* **Frank** *walks to the kitchen and opens a cupboard and sees what's there.* **Rosanna** *and* **Deanne** *plump themselves on the sofa and take their shoes off.*

**Frank**   There's rum.

**Deanne**   Rum.

**Rosanna**   Rum it is.

**Deanne**   Have you got anything else?

**Frank**   Just rum.

**Deanne**   I like rum.

**Rosanna**   Yeah *I* like rum hurry up and pour it and give it to us.

**Frank** *pulls out a bottle of rum.*

Italy are in white.

**Deanne**   I thought they play in blue?

**Rosanna**   Very good Dee.

**Frank**   Very good.

**Rosanna**   I'm impressed.

**Deanne**   You see.

**Rosanna**   Scotland play in blue so Italy are in white ain't that right Frank?

**Frank**   It is.

**Rosanna**   You see.

**Deanne**   Here where's that rum?

**Frank**   It's coming.

**Rosanna**   Blimey.

**Deanne**   Get your skates on.

**Rosanna**   What do you have to do to get a drink around here?

**Deanne**   I know.

**Rosanna**   Game over.

**Deanne**   Did Scotland win?

**Rosanna**   Italy.

**Frank**   Game over?

**Rosanna**   We're through.

**Frank**   Piece of piss.

**Rosanna**   The jocks are out.

**Deanne**   Ahh. Are they out?

**Rosanna**   They're out.

**Deanne**   Couldn't they let them in?

**Rosanna** *looks nonplussed.*

**Rosanna**   No they couldn't let them in. That's not how it works. You're either in or you're out and they're out. If they were in someone else would be out. Someone else better than them because they're shit.

**Rosanna** *cracks up.*

**Frank**   It's white.

**Rosanna**   What?

**Frank**   The rum.

**Rosanna**   White?

**Frank**   White.

**Deanne**   Is it rum?

**Frank**   Course it's rum.

**Deanne**   Well then.

**Rosanna**   I don't care if it's yellow with purple spots. If it says rum it's good enough for me.

**Deanne**   Exactly.

**Rosanna**   Italy played in white the rum's white I think I see a link.

**Rosanna** *smacks her hands together.*

This is going to be a good night.

**Frank**   What do you want it with?

**Rosanna**   What have you got?

**Frank** *opens the fridge and pulls out some apple juice.*

**Frank**   Apple.

**Rosanna**   Apple?

**Deanne**   What else?

**Frank**   Nothing.

**Rosanna** *and* **Deanne** *look nonplussed.*

My mate knows about drinks he's a drinks aficionado *he* drinks apple and rum.

**Deanne**   Does he?

**Frank**   Rum and apple he calls it.

**Rosanna**   Does he?

**Frank**   Mind you that's dark rum.

**Rosanna**   That's dark rum.

**Deanne**   This is white rum.

**Rosanna**   This is white rum.

**Deanne**   Have you got any coke?

**Rosanna**   *I've* got coke.

**Deanne**   Have you?

**Rosanna**   Frank be an angel and run next door and get the coke.

**Deanne**   Shall I?

**Rosanna**   No he'll do it.

**Frank**   Oh will I?

**Rosanna**   The door's open.

**Rosanna** *and* **Deanne** *stare at* **Frank** *as if to say 'what are you waiting for?'.*

**Frank**   What's wrong with rum and apple?

**Rosanna**   I'll tell you what's wrong with rum and apple . . .

**Deanne**   There's a *lot* wrong with it.

**Rosanna**   There's a *lot* wrong with it. First of all rum and apple ain't a drink.

**Deanne**   Rum and coke now *there's* a drink.

**Rosanna**   Rum and coke the coke's next door you go next door you fetch the coke you pour the coke in the rum you throw the apple out the window you close the fridge you shut the fuck up.

**Deanne**   I'm sorry Frank I have to side with Rosanna on this one you know I don't like to take sides.

**Rosanna**   That's right.

**Deanne**   I'm entirely impartial.

**Rosanna**   You are.

**Deanne**   I have no vested interest either way. I'm looking at this purely from a neutral perspective. I've heard your argument I've heard her argument and I have to find in favour of Rosanna. I'm sorry. It's nothing personal. Rum and apple is just a sick joke. I feel soiled just thinking about it. I want to change my clothes. I want to have a bath. I'm traumatised just by the thought. I need counselling. Shock therapy. I'm going to have to claim disability allowance. I'll never be able to walk again. Look at me. I can't get up. I'm stuck here forever. This is not good.

**Rosanna**   Be quick.

**Rosanna** *and* **Deanne** *stare at* **Frank** *as if to say 'this is an emergency'.* **Frank** *slips into his shoes and walks off through the front door.*

Good lad.

**Rosanna** *and* **Deanne** *crack up.*

**Deanne**   He's a good lad.

**Deanne** *gets up and starts making herself a rum and apple.*

**Rosanna**   So he should go next door. What does he do?
Not a lot by the look of it. Does he work?

**Deanne**   No.

**Rosanna**   No.

**Deanne**   He looks after Bubba.

**Rosanna**   That's no work for a man. Kate should be
looking after Bubba. She wants to be looking after Bubba
but she can't. She has to work.

**Deanne**   Part-time. She only works three days.

**Rosanna**   So what?

**Deanne**   She gets good money.

**Rosanna**   Working for that lunatic.

**Deanne**   He's a genius.

**Rosanna**   He's a drug addict. Don't get confused.

**Deanne**   Have you seen his clothes?

**Rosanna**   I *have* seen his clothes and they're good.

**Deanne**   He's the best.

**Rosanna**   He's the best. I won't hold that against him. But
have you heard the stories?

**Deanne**   No. Tell me.

**Rosanna**   I *will* tell you. Suffice to say your hair will stand
on end.

**Deanne**   Tell me then.

**Rosanna**   I can't tell you with Kate in the house she'll be
out any minute.

**Deanne**   She won't hear.

**Rosanna**    I'm sworn to secrecy. She told me not to tell anyone. I can hardly tell you when she's next door.

**Deanne**    Okay then whisper it.

**Deanne** *rushes over to the sofa with her drink and sits down.*

**Rosanna**    'Completely out of control'.

**Deanne**    Is it?

**Rosanna**    It is.

**Deanne**    Is he a lunatic?

**Rosanna**    He doesn't treat Katie right. He doesn't treat anyone right. He's an addict. He needs someone to clump him over the head with a bat.

**Deanne**    He's powerful though.

**Rosanna**    That's his trouble. No-one will stand up to him. Katie stands up to him but he doesn't listen. It falls on deaf ears.

**Deanne**    Then why did she go back?

**Rosanna**    He lured her back didn't he. He's quite the charmer. He trusts her. She's the only person there he trusts. She 'gets' him she fights his corner everyone else there wants to make him mass market. They don't care about the brand they only care about the dosh. She sees the bigger picture. She protects him.

**Deanne**    He's a tortured artist he needs protecting.

**Rosanna**    Don't give me all that flannel.

**Deanne**    What?

**Rosanna**    I'm going to clump you in a minute.

**Deanne**    What have I said?

**Rosanna**    He's an addict. Be-all and end-all. Tortured artist my bare arse. What's he got to be tortured about? I'll tell you who should be tortured. Nurses. They should be tortured. Up on their feet all day and all for six pounds an hour. I don't see anyone feeling sorry for them.

**Deanne**    Loads of people do.

**Rosanna**    That's not the point. They can't take three days off with a hangover.

**Deanne**    Is that what he does?

**Rosanna**    And the rest.

**Deanne**    Are you serious?

**Rosanna**    I don't see any nurses on the front of any magazines. Tortured bollocks. The only thing he has to be tortured about is how to spend all his money. *That's* what he's got to be tortured about. Don't give me all that artistic nonsense. You sound like Frank. Ooh I can't work I'm an artist. Look at me I'm so artistic. Excuse me while I go and do something arty. Bollocks. I'd love to be an artist.

**Deanne**    What can you do?

**Rosanna**    I was good at painting.

**Deanne**    Was you?

**Rosanna**    I was talented. Nothing I'd like more than to be a painter. Red yellow I can draw. Light and shade I know it all. I'd love to sit around all day saying I'm a painter. Having coffee. Some of us have kids to raise. Listen kids I'm sorry there's no food today how about I paint you some food how about I paint you a beefburger. With relish. It won't wash. Take your head out the clouds and *work*. Lazy bugger.

**Deanne**    It's hard.

**Rosanna**    Oh spare me the sob story.

**Deanne**    She has a career.

**Rosanna**    So he should rebuild *his* career and if he can't he should do something else. You started afresh. You worked hard you studied you got yourself a job.

**Deanne**  I bettered myself.

**Rosanna**  You did.

**Deanne**  No-one helped me.

**Rosanna**  Quite the contrary. You helped others. That was the whole ethos of your job. Helping others. Women in need. Like *you'd* been in need before.

**Deanne**  I taught myself to read and write. You missed that bit out.

**Rosanna**  Pardon me.

**Deanne**  No-one gave me a helping hand.

**Rosanna**  That's what I'm saying. Don't start singing your own praises that's what *I'm* doing.

**Deanne**  Oh sorry.

**Rosanna**  Blimey. Can't you take a compliment. I'm complimenting you there's no need for you to join in.

**Deanne**  I take it back.

**Rosanna**  Show a bit of humility.

**Deanne**  You're right Rose I don't know what came over me. Not many people sing my praises.

**Rosanna**  Don't start with all that.

**Deanne**  What?

**Rosanna**  I've warned you.

**Deanne**  It's true though.

**Rosanna**  That's my point. Rather than sit around bemoaning your luck you got on with it.

**Deanne**  I wouldn't go back there if you paid me.

**Rosanna**  Don't be bitter Dee. Nothing worse than being bitter.

**Deanne**   Can you blame me?

**Rosanna**   You should have gone back there.

**Deanne**   Impossible.

**Rosanna**   You should have walked straight back in with your head held high.

**Deanne**   Are you serious?

**Rosanna**   Of course I am.

**Deanne**   After what they said about me?

**Rosanna**   All of which was proved false.

**Deanne**   So what?

**Rosanna**   You leaving let them win.

**Deanne**   Let them win.

**Rosanna**   I suppose you're not afraid to start all over. I'll give you that. You're not afraid to take a menial job.

**Deanne**   I work the till Rose it ain't menial.

**Rosanna**   That's not what I'm saying.

**Deanne**   I like my job. I get to meet people. And I get twenty-five per cent off all produce.

**Rosanna**   They do good food.

**Deanne**   Have you tried their puddings?

**Rosanna**   No.

**Deanne**   You have to try their puddings. I'm not being funny but their puddings are good. That's why I mention it.

**Rosanna**   I hope you're not giving all your earnings back to them.

**Deanne**   As if.

**Rosanna**   You've got a young one to support.

**Deanne**   Not so young. He's a teenager soon.

**Rosanna**    Exactly.

**Deanne**    Secondary school.

**Rosanna**    Would you believe it?

**Deanne**    He'll have your Danny there. To look after him.

**Rosanna**    That he will.

**Deanne**    As a role model sort of thing.

**Rosanna**    That's it. You couldn't get a better role model than my Danny. Stays out of trouble. Does as he's told. He's a good boy. If your Max turns out anything like my Danny. You're laughing.

**Rosanna** *nods*.

**Deanne**    His grades are shit though.

**Rosanna**    What?

**Deanne**    I'm just saying.

**Rosanna**    They're not shit. They're below average. He's not an academic.

**Deanne**    What is he then?

**Rosanna**    Not an academic. Let's just leave it there. There's more to life than academia. Plenty more.

**Deanne**    I'm not casting aspersions.

**Rosanna**    You better not be.

**Deanne**    He does his best.

**Rosanna**    Which is more than I can say for that Frank. Good-for-nothing layabout.

**Deanne**    He gets royalties.

**Rosanna**    So what?

**Deanne**    He brings in something.

**Rosanna**    There's four mouths to feed.

**Deanne**    Chrissie ain't his.

**Rosanna**    That's another thing. Chrissie. What does *her* father do?

**Deanne**    I saw him on the telly the other day.

**Rosanna**    Prances about pretending to be a rock n roll star?

**Deanne**    He's good.

**Rosanna**    That's no job for a man.

**Deanne**    He's good though.

**Rosanna**    Who's looking after his daughter? Katie. Katie has to do everything. Why do you think she works? She's keeping everyone afloat. If it wasn't for her her children would starve. She's knackered you only have to look at her to see that. She looks like shit. Why do you think that is? She's not treated right. Why do you think *that* is? Because every bloke in her life's an artist. The three most important men in her life, other than her own flesh and blood, all artists. A writer, a fashion designer, a pop star. Don't tell me that's not fucked-up. Don't tell me that's not going to lead a woman to an early grave. Of course it is. That can't be good for anyone. Self-consumed that's what they are. Artists. That's why they're addicts. It's a disease of the self Katie told me. 'A disease of the self'. And you wonder why she has a face like a slapped arse.

**Rosanna** *nods*.

**Deanne**    I don't.

**Rosanna**    Oh come on you must have thought it.

**Deanne**    She's beautiful.

**Rosanna**    *Was* beautiful.

**Deanne**    I've never seen anyone so happy.

**Rosanna**    She's got Bubba. It's papering over the cracks. You have to wonder why she goes with them knowing they're only going to let her down. You have to wonder what that says about her self-esteem.

**Rosanna** *nods*.

**Deanne**    She doesn't know they're addicts.

**Rosanna**    What do you mean?

**Deanne**    When she meets them.

**Rosanna**    Of course she does.

**Deanne**    They don't walk around with a big sign saying addict. You should know that better than anyone.

**Rosanna**    She knows.

**Deanne**    She does not.

**Rosanna**    She can see they're on a self-destruct.

**Deanne**    Perhaps she's so taken with them she can't see anything.

**Rosanna**    Oh please.

**Deanne**    What if she thinks she can change them?

**Rosanna**    Huh?

**Deanne**    Or she thinks they'll change for her?

**Rosanna** *looks nonplussed*.

**Rosanna**    Katie?

**Deanne**    Why not?

**Rosanna**    Full of herself?

**Deanne**    Who said that?

**Rosanna**    Just because she lives in this place?

**Deanne**    What are you talking about?

**Rosanna**    Is that really what you think?

**Deanne**    You've spun my words around.

**Rosanna**   I'll give her what for if she's not careful. Turning her nose up at me. Silly tart. Fuck it I'm leaving.

**Deanne**   What?

**Rosanna**   Get your shoes on.

**Rosanna** *reaches for her shoes.*

**Deanne**   The X Factor.

**Rosanna**   Fuck The X Factor we'll watch it at my place.

**Deanne**   You haven't got a plasma.

**Rosanna**   You are such a superficial bitch do you know that?

*They both stare at* **Katie** *as she walks on through the bedroom door in her slippers. Early forties.*

**Katie**   Ladies.

**Rosanna**   Katie.

**Rosanna** *puts down her shoes.*

**Katie**   Where's Frank?

**Deanne**   Next door.

**Deanne** *gets up and starts making herself a refill.*

**Rosanna**   We thought we'd get him working for once.

**Katie**   He does a lot where it counts.

**Rosanna**   Oh yeah?

**Deanne**   Where's that?

**Katie**   Where do you think?

**Deanne**   Oh is it?

**Katie** *and* **Deanne** *laugh.*

**Rosanna**   Well I'm glad he's good for something.

**Deanne**   You're just jealous.

**Rosanna**   Damn right I'm jealous. What I wouldn't do for a good seeing to.

**Katie** *and* **Deanne** *laugh.*

I'm thinking of going on a dating site.

**Deanne**   Are you?

**Katie**   I could never do that.

**Deanne**   Lots of people do it.

**Katie**   Do they?

**Deanne**   I was reading about it.

**Rosanna**   I don't know.

**Katie**   Go on take the plunge Rose.

**Katie** *and* **Deanne** *laugh.*

We can live vicariously through you.

**Deanne**   You can have an orgy.

**Katie**   Have a sixsome.

**Deanne**   Yeah.

**Katie** *and* **Deanne** *laugh.*

**Rosanna**   I've looked into it.

**Katie**   I bet you have.

**Katie** *and* **Deanne** *laugh.*

**Rosanna**   There's plenty of sites for older men but not older women.

**Katie**   Oh crikes don't say you're old you're making *me* feel old.

**Rosanna**   You're younger than me.

**Katie**   Not saying much is it?

**Katie** *and* **Deanne** *laugh while* **Rosanna** *gives a look.*

**Rosanna**   Younger women you're fine. Men of all ages. Older women you're fucked. Unless you want to meet a young guy.

**Katie**   What's wrong with that?

**Katie** *and* **Deanne** *laugh.*

**Rosanna**   It's discriminatory.

**Deanne**   That's a long word.

**Rosanna**   Shut up. What happens if I want to meet a bloke my age?

**Katie**   You visit a morgue.

**Rosanna**   Shut up.

**Katie** *and* **Deanne** *laugh while* **Rosanna** *gives a look.*

I'm being serious. Young guys only want one thing. They don't want a relationship with an older woman. If they want a relationship they pick on someone their own age. They love an older lady. I have this on good authority.

**Katie**   Who?

**Rosanna**   Your fella.

**Katie**   You what?

**Rosanna**   Mothers I'd Like To Fuck. He told me all about it.

**Katie**   Did he?

**Rosanna**   I don't want no-strings sex.

**Katie**   Why not?

**Rosanna**   I'm not a slag. I'm not like Cheree.

**Deanne**   She's getting what she wants.

**Katie**   I'm not so sure.

**Deanne**   Some young men might want a relationship.

**Rosanna**   Then what happens? They want kids. I can't give them kids. I've got kids of my own I'm too *old* to have kids

and even if I *could* have kids I'm not having anymore. I
don't want a relationship with a young man.

**Deanne**   Old men might want kids.

**Rosanna**   They can find a younger woman. Let's face it all
they want is a younger woman that's why there's so many
sites that cater for them. It don't matter if they have kids if
they don't have kids if they're married if they're single if
they have three arms and three legs. It don't matter. There's
always a young whore willing to shag them. There's always a
young whore willing to laugh at their jokes. Jokes an older
woman's heard a million times. Older women aren't so
easily impressed. They're harder work that's their trouble.
Men don't want to work. Men don't want someone on their
level. I know men.

**Katie**   How do you know men?

**Deanne**   You've only been with one man in the last thirty
years.

**Rosanna**   And look at him.

**Katie**   You can hardly use him as the benchmark.

**Rosanna**   I want a man who's got kids and has done all
that stuff. There's not one site out there that caters for me.
Not one.

**Deanne**   You're a very specialised market.

**Katie**   That's for sure.

**Katie** *and* **Deanne** *laugh while* **Rosanna** *gives a look.*

**Rosanna**   Young men? I can find five tonight like that.

**Katie** *looks nonplussed.*

**Katie**   Why don't you?

**Katie** *and* **Deanne** *laugh.*

**Rosanna**   Silly slags.

**Deanne** *finishes her drink, leaves her glass in the kitchen, and sits back down on the sofa. They all stare at* **Frank** *as he walks on through the front door with a bottle of coke.*

**Deanne**   What took you?

**Frank**   Who's that friend of Danny's?

**Rosanna**   What about him?

**Frank**   What's his name?

**Rosanna**   Spark. Why?

**Frank**   Spark?

**Rosanna**   That's his name.

**Frank**   That's his name?

**Rosanna**   He's called Spark.

**Frank**   That's not his real name.

**Rosanna**   Whatever.

**Frank**   Spark?

**Frank** *looks nonplussed.*

**Rosanna**   What about him?

**Frank**   When I went in it was dark outside . . .

**Rosanna**   Well it *is* dark outside.

**Frank**   And the light was on in the hall and he had just come out of the toilet and he was looking at himself in the mirror.

**Rosanna**   So what?

**Frank**   Well he couldn't see me but I could see him. You know that way teenagers look at themselves in the mirror. He was taking ages. In the end I just had to go in. I pretended I hadn't been watching him for the past fifteen minutes.

**Rosanna**   What did he do?

**Frank**   What could he do he said hello.

**Deanne**   Ahh bless.

**Frank**   He acted like he hadn't just been caught doing John Travolta impressions.

**Deanne** *cracks up.*

I've never seen so much acne in my life.

**Deanne**   Ahh bless.

**Frank**   I said nothing. I could have mentioned the fact John Travolta doesn't have acne but I thought why, what good will it do? If he wants to look like John Travolta in the mirror who am I to burst his bubble? If he thinks he's John Travolta – fine – no sweat off my nose. I'd rather he didn't leave me outside looking through the door whilst he gave his little performance but other than that he can do what he wants. I'm not his mother. If I was his mother I'd ban all mirrors from the house. And anything to do with John Travolta. Kid's deluded.

**Katie**   It can't be easy being that spotty.

**Frank**   Have you seen him?

**Katie**   No.

**Frank**   It ain't easy believe me. There's more spots on him than A Hundred And One Dalmatians. The sooner he knocks off all that John Travolta stuff the better. He can get on with his life. Hiya babe.

**Katie**   Hiya.

**Frank**   How's the Bubs?

**Frank** *slips out of his shoes.*

**Katie**   Beautiful.

**Rosanna**   Little munchkin how is he?

**Katie**   Beautiful.

**Deanne**    Is he good Kate?

**Katie**    He's well.

**Deanne**    Ahh bless.

**Rosanna**    He's beautiful that's what he is.

*The entry phone goes.*

Who's that?

**Frank**    Takeaway.

**Rosanna**    What you having?

**Frank**    Indian.

**Katie** *answers the entry phone.*

**Katie**    Hello? Coming down.

**Rosanna**    Why don't you go down Frank?

**Frank**    What?

**Rosanna**    Go down and fetch the takeaway. Here Katie why don't you have a drink.

**Katie**    I can't I'm breastfeeding.

**Rosanna**    One won't kill you.

**Katie**    I'm fine.

**Rosanna** *stares at* **Frank** *as if to say 'what are you waiting for?'.*

**Rosanna**    See ya.

**Frank** *hands* **Katie** *the coke, slips into his shoes, and walks off through the front door.* **Deanne** *gets up, takes the coke off* **Katie**, *takes her glass, and starts making herself a rum and coke.* **Katie** *follows her to the kitchen and starts pulling out two plates, two forks, and spoons to serve with.*

**Katie**    You're a bit hard on him Rose.

**Rosanna**    Who?

**Katie**  Frank.

**Rosanna**  Hard on him?

**Deanne**  Yeah you are.

**Rosanna**  What am I hard on him for?

**Deanne**  He does his best.

**Rosanna**  He's a drug addict.

**Katie**  He's a *recovering* drug addict.

**Rosanna**  Recovering my arse.

**Katie**  Why don't you give him a chance he's not like your Jimmy he recognises he suffers from something and he does something about it.

**Rosanna**  Suffers from what?

**Katie**  A disease.

**Rosanna**  Do me a favour. You see my Jack? He has a disease. He has to take medication. He has to go to hospital for check-ups. My little darling boy. Your Frank suffers from nothing more than the fact he chose to take too many drugs and then found out he couldn't stop.

**Katie**  It's not as simple as that. If you went to meetings you'd understand.

**Rosanna**  Why should I go to meetings?

**Katie**  To understand Jimmy.

**Rosanna**  Why should I understand Jimmy?

**Katie**  To help you accept.

**Rosanna**  Why can't anyone understand me? Why's everyone's got to understand him? What about me? Did I walk out on him and leave my two children and never contribute a penny to their upbringing? Was that me?

**Katie**  He's in a bad way.

**Rosanna**   What about me? Who has to pick up the pieces? Who cooks their dinner and washes their clothes? And works. And drives them around. I can't fanny about free of responsibility. I'd love to have a life like him.

**Katie**   You wouldn't, believe me.

**Rosanna**   Do me a favour. He has it cushty.

**Deanne** *finishes her drink, leaves her glass in the kitchen, and sits back down on the sofa. They all stare at* **Frank** *as he walks on through the front door with the takeaway.*

**Frank**   Who has it cushty?

**Deanne**   Her Jimmy.

**Frank**   On to that.

**Rosanna**   She started it.

**Frank**   What's he done this time?

**Rosanna**   I'll tell you what he *hasn't* done. He hasn't picked up his kids when he said he was going to. He hasn't cooked them any meals or given them any money. He's got money for coke but not for them. In fact I can't think of a single *thing* he's done.

**Frank**   You need to go to meetings.

**Rosanna**   Fuck off.

**Frank**   You'd be less resentful.

**Rosanna**   Why *shouldn't* I be resentful?

**Frank**   Because it doesn't help you. Simple as. It doesn't help those around you. Resentment corrodes. It blocks you from your spirit.

**Rosanna**   I'd be less resentful if you stopped talking so much bollocks. If he paid a bit of maintenance. *Then* I'd be less resentful.

**Frank**   You can't change him. You can only change you. Stop waiting for him to solve his problems and start solving yours.

**Rosanna**   *He's* my problem. I wouldn't have any problems if it wasn't for him. I had a good man everything would be okay.

**Katie**   You'll never find anyone until you sort out your stuff. And even if you *did* find someone your stuff will still *be* there.

**Frank**   Is a man an answer to all your woes?

**Rosanna**   I haven't had sex in over three years. You don't think a man would solve a few things? *I* certainly do. There's only so much you can do on your own. Do you know what I mean? I don't want to get too graphic.

**Frank**   No.

**Rosanna**   A man might not solve everything but he'd certainly solve a major fucking issue.

**Rosanna** *nudges* **Deanne**.

Hey Dee?

**Rosanna** *cracks up*.

**Frank**   Nothing can fix you except you. You have to be willing.

**Rosanna**   Why can't *he* be willing?

**Frank**   Maybe he will be one day. I hope so. Otherwise he's doomed.

**Rosanna**   Yeah let's all feel sorry for him a bit more. Let's all get on our knees and pray for him. Poor soul. It's a hard life. Let's all have a whip-round and send him the proceeds so he can put it all up his nose. That's a good idea. Crikey I feel like I've joined the Mormons. Put on The X Factor.

**Deanne**   Has it started?

**Rosanna**   It's about to.

**Deanne** *changes the channel with the remote.* **Katie** *takes the takeaway off* **Frank** *and starts serving up the food while he slips out of his shoes.*

**Deanne** I'm not being funny but I've been here twenty fucking minutes and I haven't even had a drink. Will someone get me a drink.

**Rosanna**    Yeah Frank why don't you get us a drink.

**Deanne**    Will you get us a drink.

**Rosanna**    The X Factor's about to start.

**Deanne**    The X Factor's about to start.

**Rosanna**    Any minute.

**Deanne**    Any minute. Here I am. Drinkless. Is that acceptable to you? Is that how you want to be remembered? As the person who watched as I died of thirst? I'd be pretty ashamed if I were you Frank. I'd take a good look at myself. Twenty minutes I've been here.

**Rosanna**    Longer.

**Deanne**    Half an hour.

**Rosanna**    Half an hour without a drink.

**Deanne**    How would *you* feel?

**Rosanna**    Thirsty. That's how you'd feel.

**Deanne**    Resentful.

**Rosanna**    Indeed.

**Frank**    Would you like a drink Dee?

**Deanne**    That would be most kind.

**Frank**    What would you like?

**Deanne**    Rum and coke.

**Rosanna**    And one for me.

**Deanne**    And one for her.

**Rosanna**    And one for me.

**Deanne**    And don't skimp on the rum either.

**Rosanna**   I only want a small one.

**Deanne**   I want a *large* one. That's that. It's non-negotiable.

**Frank**   Coming up.

**Frank** *starts making two rum and cokes.*

**Deanne**   Have a large one Rose.

**Rosanna**   Nah.

**Deanne**   Go on.

**Rosanna**   I said no.

**Deanne**   Let your hair down.

**Rosanna**   I'm alright.

**Deanne**   Go crazy.

**Rosanna**   Will you fuck off.

**Deanne**   What are you scared of?

**Rosanna**   I'm not scared of anything I just want a small one.

**Deanne**   Why don't you have a large one?

**Rosanna**   Why don't *you* have a large one?

**Deanne**   I *am* having a large one.

**Rosanna**   Well why don't you have a *larger* one?

**Deanne**   Frank make that a larger one.

**Rosanna** *and* **Deanne** *crack up.* **Katie** *puts a plate of food and a fork down on the coffee table for* **Frank**. *She sits down on the armchair beside the sofa with her own plate of food and a fork and starts eating.*

**Katie**   Are either of you hungry?

**Deanne**   No I'm not.

**Rosanna**   We've had dinner.

**Deanne**   Why, is there more?

**Katie**    There's some on the side.

**Deanne**    Are you sure it's going spare?

**Katie**    Well it is if Frank doesn't want it.

**Deanne**    Do you want it Frank?

**Frank**    Want what?

**Deanne**    Your food.

**Frank**    No you can have it.

**Deanne** *gets up and starts serving herself some food.* **Frank** *gives her her drink in a new glass.*

**Deanne**    Aah thanks.

**Frank** *gives* **Rosanna** *her drink.*

**Rosanna**    No ice?

**Frank**    What?

**Rosanna**    Ice.

**Deanne**    The X Factor's about to start.

**Rosanna**    Rum and coke with ice I said.

**Frank**    Have we got ice?

**Katie**    No.

**Rosanna**    You haven't got ice?

**Deanne**    No ice?

**Katie**    The ice maker's broken.

**Frank**    We need to get it fixed.

**Rosanna**    What do you mean we need to get it fixed?

**Katie**    We need to get some ice trays.

**Rosanna**    Who's we?

**Frank**    Me.

**Rosanna**   That's better.

**Deanne**   No ice? That's really spoiled my night that has. Honestly you couldn't make it up. If I were to tell someone what happened tonight no-one would believe me. First no-one gave me a drink. Three hours I waited. Then when the drink *did* finally arrive there was no coke. Then when the *coke* finally arrived there was no ice. Next you'll be telling me there's no bar snacks.

**Frank**   What?

**Deanne**   Bar snacks.

**Frank** *looks nonplussed.*

**Frank**   What do you want bar snacks for?

**Deanne**   Nibbles.

**Frank**   You're nibbling my fucking curry.

**Deanne** *looks nonplussed.*

**Deanne**   He just don't get it.

**Deanne** *leaves her untouched drink in the kitchen and sits back down on the sofa with her plate of food and a fork.*

**Rosanna**   I've got ice next door.

**Frank**   What?

**Rosanna**   You heard.

**Deanne**   Frank be an angel. I can't drink rum and coke without ice.

**Rosanna**   You heard the woman.

**Deanne**   Rum and coke without ice. I haven't done that since. I don't know when.

**Katie**   Since before ice was invented.

**Deanne**   Oi I'm not that old.

**Katie** *and* **Deanne** *laugh.*

I might be old Kate but I'm not that old.

**Rosanna**   It's open.

**Frank**   What?

**Rosanna**   My house. You know where the fridge is. Open the fridge the freezer's on top. Open the freezer you'll find some ice. Bring the ice put the ice in the drinks put the rest of the ice in your freezer that way the ice won't melt and next time you make us a drink you'll be able to put ice in it. Ain't that right?

**Deanne**   That's right.

**Rosanna**   It sounds right from where I'm sitting.

**Deanne**   From where I'm sitting too.

**Rosanna** and **Deanne** *stare at* **Frank** *as if to say 'what are you waiting for?'.*

**Rosanna**   Well?

**Frank**   But my food's getting cold.

**Deanne**   His food's getting cold.

**Rosanna**   The sooner you get back the hotter it will be.

**Frank**   Kate.

**Rosanna**   Don't Kate.

**Frank**   My food.

**Rosanna**   'His food'.

**Frank** *considers what to do, slips into his shoes, and rushes off through the front door.*

**Katie**   You two need to lay off him.

**Rosanna** *cracks up.*

Seriously.

**Deanne** *gets up and starts adding more food to her untouched plate as well as picking from the containers. Until such time as*

**Frank** *returns, she continues eating and drinking and refilling her glass.*

**Deanne**    I've got bad news.

**Rosanna**    What?

**Deanne**    I'm so upset I can't talk about it.

**Katie**    Talk about it.

**Rosanna**    A problem shared is a problem . . .

**Rosanna** *can't find the end of the saying.*

Talk about it.

**Deanne**    Reginald.

**Katie**    Reggie?

**Rosanna**    What about him?

**Deanne**    Diabetes.

**Katie**    No?

**Rosanna**    When did you find this out?

**Deanne**    Yesterday.

**Rosanna**    You never said.

**Deanne**    He could go blind Rose. He has to take insulin. Regularly. He has to watch his sugar levels. My Reggie. You know how he likes sugar. You've seen the size of him.

**Rosanna**    That's the trouble. His weight.

**Katie**    He ain't that fat.

**Deanne**    Have you seen his belly?

**Katie**    No.

**Deanne**    He keeps it well hidden. For good reason.

**Rosanna**    His dad was fat.

**Deanne**   Weren't he just.

**Rosanna**   You're not exactly skinny.

**Deanne**   Oi.

**Katie**   The party's over Dee.

**Deanne**   I know. He's only twenty-six.

**Katie**   He does like to burn the candle at both ends.

**Deanne**   I know. I told him, that's all over. The drinking.

**Katie**   Does he take drugs?

**Deanne**   No.

**Rosanna**   You wouldn't know anyway.

**Deanne**   I would so.

**Rosanna**   You wouldn't. I speak from experience. Tell her Kate.

**Katie**   It's true.

**Rosanna**   I wouldn't have known if I hadn't have gone through Jim's pockets. He was doing it in secret.

**Katie**   That's the nature of addiction.

**Rosanna**   Ask Kate. She's an expert on the subject. She's had more addicts than I've had leg waxes.

**Katie**   What does *that* mean?

**Rosanna**   Every bloke you've ever had has been an addict.

**Katie** *thinks about it*.

**Katie**   That's true.

**Katie** *laughs*.

**Rosanna**   Addicted to addicts.

**Katie**   Co-dependent.

**Rosanna**    Don't give me all that mumbo jumbo. You like addicts.

**Deanne**    They like you.

**Rosanna**    Look at Zane. *He's* an addict.

**Katie** *doesn't answer.*

He's still out there. 'Doing it'.

**Katie** *doesn't answer.*

Well then. Total liability. Waste of flipping space. Never mind the fact he's a pop star what about his daughter.

**Katie**    He's good with her.

**Rosanna**    Does he meet his responsibilities?

**Katie**    He does what he can.

**Rosanna**    Bollocks.

**Katie**    Look Rose. What's the point me stewing over what he doesn't do? How does that help me? I accepted he was ill long ago. Expectation only leads to anger.

**Rosanna**    You have a right to expect him to *care* about her.

**Katie**    He *does* care about her.

**Rosanna**    Oh really?

**Katie**    Yeah.

**Rosanna**    Isn't it you that says love is a doing word?

**Katie**    What?

**Rosanna**    You heard.

**Katie** *looks nonplussed.*

**Katie**    He does what he can. What he's capable of.

**Rosanna**    He's a weasel.

**Katie**    He's ill.

**Rosanna**    If being a weasel is an illness well that lets an awful lot of arseholes off the hook.

**Katie**    Why you so concerned about him?

**Rosanna**    I'm not.

**Katie**    I can sit in resentment or I can get on with my life. I choose to get on with my life.

**Rosanna**    By being with another addict.

**Katie**    Those addicts you speak of have no choice in the matter. Just like an epileptic has no choice over that. Or a diabetic.

**Deanne**    Don't mind me.

**Katie**    Sorry Dee.

**Deanne**    I'm only at my wits' end over here.

**Katie**    Sorry Dee.

**Deanne**    About to top myself.

**Rosanna**    Diabetics don't ruin the lives of those around them. I don't know how you can even compare them. Reggie's done nothing wrong. What's an epileptic got to do with anything?

**Katie**    I take my *own* inventory I don't take theirs. The fact that I go with addicts is *my* look-out you're right. That's not *their* fault. Just like *your* problems aren't Jimmy's fault.

**Rosanna**    I'll tell you something for nothing. The next guy I get with ain't going to be an addict. I've had it with addicts. One was enough for me.

**Katie**    Yes addicts destroy the lives of those around them but they're not responsible for your response. *You're* responsible for that.

**Rosanna**    I'm responsible but he's not?

**Katie**    If I was with a bull and the bull smashed all the china I can hardly blame the bull. I don't have to *like* the bull but I can hardly blame him. The bull's a bull.

**Rosanna**    A leopard can't change its spots.

**Katie**    That's where you're wrong.

**Rosanna**    Next man's going to be a real man. Not someone I have to mother. Someone who can look after *me*.

**Katie**    Good luck.

**Deanne**    If he has a brother let me know.

**Deanne** *waits for a response but none comes.*

Did you not hear that I thought that was quite a good quip . . . If he has a brother . . . No?

**Deanne** *shuts up and they all gaze at the telly.*

**Katie**    If I had remained angry at Zane I wouldn't have met Frank or I'd have put too many expectations upon him and I wouldn't have Bubbalicious.

**Deanne**    Ahh.

**Rosanna**    Little munchkin.

**Deanne**    He's beautiful.

**Katie**    He's a treasure.

**Rosanna**    You got lucky. That has nothing to do with planning.

**Deanne**    Lucky?

**Katie**    I thought I should never have gone near Frank?

**Rosanna**    He's alright. Bit lazy but we'll let that go. He makes me laugh.

**Deanne**    He makes *me* laugh.

**Rosanna**    He's not a bad sort.

**Katie**    That's cos he's sorting himself out. Changing his 'spots'.

**Rosanna**    He's a long way to go yet Kate.

**Katie**   I know that. But I'm willing to give him a chance. What's the alternative? He's Bubba's father.

**Deanne**   He's a great dad.

**Katie**   He's the best.

**Deanne**   That boy loves him. You're lucky there.

**Rosanna**   Ain't she just.

**Katie**   Why dwell on the things he doesn't do why not dwell on what he does? Lord knows I nag enough but what does it change? Only *he* can change himself and he's changing.

**Rosanna**   How's he changing?

**Katie**   Does he rant and rave? Sneak out and not come back? Say one thing and do another? He goes to bed early he gets up early. Opens his mail. *Does things*. It may not sound a lot to you but to an addict, it's progress. It shows he's on the right path.

**Rosanna**   You're too easy on him.

**Katie**   You're too hard on Jim.

**Rosanna** *scoffs*.

He's gone. Leave it there.

**Rosanna**   How can I leave it there he's my kids' fucking father?

**Deanne**   No-one does drugs in my family I don't know what you're talking about.

**Katie** *and* **Rosanna** *look nonplussed*.

**Katie**   Huh?

**Deanne**   How can you even *imply* my Reggie does drugs?

**Rosanna**   No-one?

**Deanne**   Vic doesn't do them he only sells them.

**Rosanna**   And that's okay?

**Katie**   No it's not.

**Rosanna**   That's worse. Rather than ruin your own life as well as everyone else's you just ruin everyone else's and get rich in the process.

**Deanne**   Whatever. He's paid his dues. He's out now.

**Katie**   How long's he been out?

**Deanne**   Two weeks.

**Katie**   And what's he doing?

**Deanne**   Don't know haven't seen him.

**Katie**   You haven't seen him?

**Deanne**   He hasn't been home since he got out.

**Katie**   Oh Dee.

**Deanne**   I know. My own son. He's still a teen. Not even a man. I worry about him so.

**Katie**   Of course you do.

**Deanne**   What set him off?

**Rosanna**   We know what set him off. It was when he found out your Joe wasn't his father. That's what set him off. Let's not beat around the bush. I know your reasons Dee and I'm not saying you did wrong but he hasn't been the same since.

**Deanne**   He hasn't been the same since.

**Rosanna**   He was such a lovely boy remember?

**Deanne**   I do.

**Rosanna**   He turned overnight.

**Deanne**   He did.

**Rosanna**   Doesn't even talk to you now.

**Deanne**   Yeah alright.

**Katie**   Don't rub it in Rose.

**Rosanna**   I'm not rubbing it in. I'm just saying.

**Katie**   Where's he staying?

**Deanne**   With his girlfriend.

**Katie**   Which one?

**Deanne**   Exactly.

**Rosanna**   The one he has a child with.

**Deanne**   That one.

**Rosanna**   Is it any wonder he sells drugs?

**Deanne**   He has mouths to feed.

**Rosanna**   What else can he do?

**Deanne**   He can go legit.

**Rosanna**   Do me a favour. All that boy's ever known is crime. What, is he suddenly going to become a nuclear physicist?

**Deanne**   He could get a job at Asda.

**Rosanna**   Stacking shelves?

**Deanne**   I work at Marks and Spencer.

**Rosanna**   That's you. Kids are different these days. They don't want to know about work. About feeding their family. About earning an honest crust. Why should they when they haven't been set an example? When their dads are either absent or if they *aren't* absent they'd far rather they were. Your kids don't know their dads. They're the lucky ones. Look at our kids. They *know* their dads. What sort of impression is that having? What sort of affect? Look at my Jim. Never done an honest day's work in his life.

**Katie**   That's not true he was fine before the drugs kicked in.

**Rosanna**   *Since* the drugs I mean. Cocaine. Sorry I'm not working anymore.

**Katie**   It's called unmanageability.

**Rosanna**   Bone idle if you ask me.

**Deanne**   I hope Vic's learned his lesson this time.

**Rosanna**   Yeah right.

**Katie**   It's possible.

**Rosanna**   A leopard can't change its spots. You might think your Frank has sorted himself out. He's only that far away from it all going down the toilet. And when it does, *you'll* be paying the consequences, not him. He'll be up and running.

**Katie**   Where is Frank?

**Rosanna**   You see.

**Katie**   His food's getting cold.

**Deanne**   Call him.

**Katie**   It's not like him to do this.

**Rosanna**   You see.

**Katie**   He's usually so reliable.

**Rosanna**   I told you.

**Katie** *makes a call from her mobile.* **Frank***'s ringtone goes. He's left his phone in the flat. A cold chill goes down* **Katie***'s spine.*

**Deanne**   He's fine he's next door.

**Katie**   Do you think so?

**Deanne**   Go down and check.

**Katie**   I can't he'll think I'm checking on him.

**Deanne**   You *are* checking on him.

**Katie**   I don't want *him* to know that.

**Deanne**   Why not?

**Katie**   I don't want to be that sort of person. One that lives in fear of their husband going off the rails. It's not good for me. It's not good for him.

**Rosanna**   Are you serious? You don't want him to know you're checking on him? For fuck sake Kate that's the only thing that will keep him in tow.

**Katie**   It's not, that's more likely to make him deviate.

**Rosanna**   I can't believe I'm hearing this.

**Katie**   It's true. It's not good for me.

**Rosanna**   Why's it not good for you?

**Katie**   That's all there is to it.

**Rosanna**   Peace of mind.

**Katie**   My peace of mind shouldn't be dependent on having him allay my fears. They're *my* fears. Not his.

**Rosanna**   You're a sucker.

**Katie**   It's my issue not his. Why should I inflict that on him? Why should I inflict it on myself? I need to trust, Frank's proved I can trust him, why should I spend my life *dis*trusting him?

**Rosanna**   Two reasons. One he's a man. Two he's an addict. Three he's got form.

**Katie**   Not anymore. He doesn't need me on his back all the time.

**Rosanna**   You want ice.

**Katie**   I don't want ice. *You* want ice. You want to know where he is go see.

**Rosanna**   He'll think you put me up to it.

**Katie**   Not my look-out.

**Rosanna**   I know what this is about.

**Katie**   What?

**Rosanna**   Zane.

**Katie** *doesn't answer.*

Cheated on you. Come on admit it. He cheated on you.

**Deanne**   Is it true Kate?

**Katie**   Who says?

**Rosanna**   He cheated on you and you're damaged by it.

**Katie**   You mean you've known all this time?

**Rosanna**   Everyone does.

**Katie** *composes herself and puts her unfinished plate down on the coffee table.*

I'm not having a pop at you babe.

**Katie**   You are.

**Rosanna**   I'm not. Honestly I'm not. I'm not trying to hurt you.

**Deanne**   Stop hurting her.

**Rosanna**   I'm saying it as it is. He cheated. You can't trust. You force yourself to trust. It drives you mad. Am I warm? Meanwhile you give your man a free rein.

**Katie**   How do you know?

**Rosanna**   Nothing gets past me babe.

**Katie**   But he was abroad.

**Rosanna**   I could tell. I'm not as stupid as you think.

**Katie**   How could you tell?

**Rosanna**   Something changed between you. Believe it or not you seemed resentful. Can't think why I mean he only went and played the field.

**Katie**   It was only once.

**Rosanna**   Who was it with?

**Katie**   No matter.

**Deanne**   Oh go on Kate tell us.

**Katie**   I bet you had a field day.

**Rosanna**   Quite the contrary. I never liked Zane. As far as I'm concerned you should have got shot long before. Totally immersed in himself.

**Katie**   I bet you've told everyone.

**Rosanna**   Not a dickybird. Discretion is the better part . . .

**Rosanna** *can't find the end of the saying.*

**Katie**   As if.

**Katie** *smirks.*

Deanne?

**Deanne**   I didn't know anything about it. Well maybe.

**Katie**   How humiliating.

**Rosanna**   Listen to me and listen to me good. You keep your eyes peeled.

**Katie**   Why, what do you know?

**Rosanna**   I don't know anything.

**Katie**   You promise me?

**Rosanna**   Do you think I wouldn't tell you? My loyalty's to you I don't know Frank from Adam.

**Katie**   I'm being paranoid. Look you've got me questioning him. Look what you're trying to do you're trying to destroy my relationship.

**Rosanna**   I'm doing no such thing.

**Katie**   You are. I'm fine with Frank. Me and Frank leave outside stuff outside our relationship. That's why we go to meetings. To remind ourselves what belongs elsewhere. I've seen women who keep their men on a tight leash. Who won't let them out of their sight. I don't want to be like them. What sort of way is that to live? Constantly panicked. Sifting through their pockets. Their mobiles.

**Rosanna**   If I hadn't have gone through Jim's pockets I wouldn't have known.

**Katie**   That's different.

**Rosanna**   Why?

**Katie**   You had reason to suspect.

**Rosanna**   Why did I?

**Katie**   I don't know you tell me. What was he doing? He was in active addiction so he must have been doing all sorts of things. Frank's in recovery.

**Rosanna**   How do you know unless you check up on him?

**Katie**   Have you seen him lately?

**Rosanna**   Yeah.

**Katie**   *That's* how I know.

**Rosanna** *chuckles.*

**Rosanna**   Addicts are clever.

**Katie**   They're not that clever. He was unmanageable now he's manageable. How did that happen?

**Rosanna**   It could all be an act.

**Katie** *frowns.*

You could be in denial.

**Katie** *nods.*

Well then.

**Katie**   Only difference is I've seen the transformation. With these eyes. I was watching him. Like a hawk. He took it. He didn't complain because he had bad credit. I got to know him in his madness and I've heard the stories. From him from others as well. I knew what he was because he told me. I had no illusions about what I was letting myself in for.

**Rosanna**   And when he lied?

**Katie**   As he did.

**Rosanna**   You gave him another chance.

**Katie**   That's part of my illness I'll admit it. Co-dependent.

**Rosanna**   You should have told him to sling his hook.

**Katie**   Whatever. How I respond is down to me. Nobody else. I certainly won't be blaming him if things go tits up. Blaming others is unhelpful. It's comforting. Sure. But unhelpful. Besides we wouldn't have Bubba.

**Deanne**   Ahh bless.

**Rosanna**   Little munchkin.

**Deanne**   How is he?

**Katie**   He's doing well Deanne thanks.

**Rosanna**   I want to grab his little cheeks and . . .

**Rosanna** *grabs an imaginary pair of cheeks and squeezes them.*

**Katie**   He smiles when he sees Frank. Do you know that? I only have to see how he responds when he sees Frank to see how Frank's doing. Frank's rebuilding his life and meanwhile, he's giving that boy a good service. That boy don't just love him he trusts him. Frank don't just love him, he *does*. Love is a doing word.

**Rosanna**   If it's such a doing word what's he doing right now? As we speak?

**Katie** *doesn't answer.*

Too trusting you, always been your problem.

**Katie**   Wrong. My problem's been the exact opposite. I've
had my trust broken. I never let my guard down again.
Frank's taught me how to. And I thank him for that. I thank
him for a whole host of stuff. For teaching me to love again.
For teaching me to put my needs ahead of my daughter's.
For once. I never put my needs above anyone's. Do you know
that? I'm co-dependent. That's why I always seek people I
can save. That's not good for me. What happens to me? I get
lost in all of it. That's what happens. My needs get put on the
back-burner. Well it may have taken an addict to convince me
to be selfish for once, but at least I got convinced, and that's a
start isn't it? Who else would have worked as hard as him? I
was hard work. I didn't return his phone calls for two years. I
gave him the brush-off time after time. Wasn't interested. He
kept coming back. Nothing put him off. Nothing. He was
compelled. Obsessed. I should have seen the warning signs
right there. Addict. It was obvious. No matter how many
things I put in his path, he kept coming back. Anyone else
would have been put off, assumed I wasn't interested. Not
him. He had a whole wall he had to break through. He broke
through it. Determined little fucker. That's why I gave him a
chance. When he puts his mind to something, he's in with a
fighting chance. I believe in him, or I *learnt* to believe in him.
Maybe I'm a fool. Who knows? It certainly hasn't been easy.
But a life lived with a closed heart is no life at all. And a life
solely thinking of others is no life either. So I'm indebted to
Frank, even if he's more indebted to me. I've set a good
example to Chrissie. Even if she doesn't know it. Do you
think she wanted him around she didn't want him around
she dotes on her father you know that. I had to let her down.
I had to tell her I'd moved on and things were going to
change. Ultimately that's better for her. Frank helped me do
that. It's difficult they don't always get on but it's worth it.
The benefits are incalculable. And you can see how much
happier she is now that Bubba's born. It's the best thing that's
ever happened to her. She had so much love to give and now
she's giving it. The day I told her I was pregnant she cried.
First one man invades her life and no sooner does she get

used to that than another one comes along too. That's the hardest thing I've ever done and I've had to do some hard things believe me. Far more than you'll ever know because I don't shoot my mouth off every two minutes. Have you any idea what I've been through?

**Rosanna**    I've got a fair idea yeah.

**Katie**    What do you mean?

**Rosanna**    You've probably been through a lot. It doesn't take a genius to work that out.

**Katie**    What do you mean?

**Rosanna**    You know what I mean. You're addicted to addicts. You said so yourself.

**Katie**    So what?

**Rosanna**    Don't get defensive.

**Katie**    I'm not.

**Rosanna**    You are. If you've done so much work on yourself how come you keep repeating the same mistakes? That's what I want to know. That's what fascinates me. What are these meetings good for?

**Katie** *doesn't answer.*

You keep telling me to go to meetings. What are they good for?

**Katie** *doesn't answer.*

Show me the evidence.

**Katie**    I don't go.

**Rosanna**    Why not?

**Katie**    Bubba.

**Rosanna**    You see. Work. Family. Eastenders. No wonder you've no time to make improvements. Not for me thank you.

You may know it all Katie but that doesn't mean you actually put it into practice. You *can't* put it into practice because you're with an addict and that addict doesn't do anything hence the reason you have no time. Do you see? If you had time you'd make the progress and you'd be able to stop yourself going with addicts and doing everything for them. Instead you're doing everything for them and you don't have time. Brilliant. That's right isn't it? What would they tell you at these meetings? About Frank? What would they tell you? Perhaps you don't want to hear it. Perhaps that's the real reason you don't go. Huh? Anyone can make time if they want to. If they really want to. Perhaps you don't have the balls.

**Katie**  I'd be given tools.

**Rosanna**  Tools for what?

**Katie**  To get through it.

**Rosanna**  Through what?

**Katie**  To serve him right through his recovery. To do the right thing. To understand what's good for both of us and what's not.

**Rosanna**  The only tool you need is a hammer to whack him over the head with. New locks on the doors. *That's* what you need.

**Katie**  I intend to go back. Okay?

**Rosanna**  It ain't meetings you need it's a fucking health farm. Look at you. You're worn out.

**Katie**  I am not.

**Rosanna** *smirks*.

**Rosanna**  Look at you.

**Katie**  What about me?

**Rosanna** *doesn't answer*.

Deanne?

**Deanne**    You look great Kate.

**Katie**    I do not.

**Deanne** You do.

**Katie**    I look shit.

**Katie** *begins to cry.*

**Rosanna**    It's okay.

**Deanne**    Rose look what you've done.

**Rosanna**    Me? I'm the one trying to help her. Come here Kate.

**Rosanna** *gets up and wipes* **Katie**'s *eyes.*

**Katie**    Get off.

**Rosanna** *looks nonplussed.*

**Rosanna**    I'm only helping you.

**Katie**    You are not. You're picking on me.

**Rosanna**    I'm trying to help you. I'm trying to make you see what's going on.

**Katie**    *Nothing's* going on.

**Rosanna**    Fine. I'll leave it.

**Rosanna** *sits back down.*

**Katie**    I'm not like you Rosie. Your Jimmy dominates every aspect of your waking life. I could be like you. But I chose not to. Simple. I chose to accept it. I chose to come to terms with it. Not to blame him but to look for my part in it. That's why I've managed to move forward and you just get angrier and angrier by the day.

**Rosanna**    Move forward? Having a man and having another child ain't moving forward. It's doing the same thing again. Bailing him out and forgiving him every time he fucks up? That's not moving forward Katie. That's bullshit. Moving forward would be being with someone who doesn't depend on you. Or being with no-one at all. No Zane no Frankie. No-one. Like me. *That's* moving forward. Having the courage of your conviction. Saying you know what, I'm better than that. I'm not putting up with that shit any more. *That's* moving forward.

**Katie**   Sitting there stewing in resentment?

**Rosanna**   Refusing to be taken for a ride again.

**Katie**   Putting up a wall to the world and not letting anything penetrate?

**Rosanna**   Not letting anything shit take the piss.

**Katie**   Not letting your heart be prised open?

**Rosanna**   Oh the joy.

**Katie**   You should let your defences down once in a while.

**Rosanna**   You should go next door Kate. You're scared out of your wits.

**Katie**   I am not.

**Rosanna**   Better him be in dread than you.

**Katie**   I'm *not* in dread.

**Rosanna** *scoffs. They all gaze at the telly.*

Here you don't think . . . ?

**Rosanna**   Has he done it before?

**Katie**   Before Bubba was born yeah. In the old days.

**Rosanna**   Disappeared for days on end.

**Katie**   He's in recovery. He's in the rooms. He has a programme.

**Rosanna**   Yeah and he's been gone half an hour. Fetching 'ice'. What's the chances when he comes back he has some cock and bull story about where he's been? He'll say he's been

talking to Dan. And John Travolta. Mentoring them in the
ways of the world. Like two teenagers have got anything to
learn from him. Some good-for-nothing lowlife who only
knows how to take drugs. Christ he don't half give himself
graces. Telling me to go to the rooms who does he think he is.

**Katie**   Leave off.

**Rosanna**   And all the while he's been down the dealer's
house.

**Katie**   He doesn't do that anymore.

**Rosanna**   Your Victor most probably. Do you see the irony?

**Deanne**   What irony?

**Rosanna**   He doesn't feed his *own* family he feeds your
son's. Do you see that?

**Katie**   You've gone on a flight of fancy.

**Rosanna**   Where is he?

**Katie**   Next door.

**Rosanna**   Call next door.

**Katie**   No.

**Rosanna**   When he gets back he'll have drugs in his pocket.
He'll have lost his appetite. Just you watch.

*They all gaze at the telly.*

**Katie**   He doesn't even have his phone on him.

**Rosanna** *looks nonplussed.*

**Rosanna**   So what?

**Katie**   How can he score drugs?

**Rosanna**   You think he needs his phone to score drugs? Do
you really think that? Not even *Deanne*'s that stupid.

**Deanne**   Oi.

**Rosanna**   He's left his phone here so you don't suspect him. Imagine you called him and he ignored it then you'd be *really* suspicious.

**Deanne** *looks nonplussed.*

Do you see?

**Deanne**   Oh yeah.

**Katie**   Don't you start.

**Deanne**   Clever.

**Rosanna**   Ingenious.

**Deanne**   You have to doff your cap to him.

**Katie**   Are you crazy?

**Deanne**   Fucking clever so-and-so.

**Katie**   If Frank was going to relapse he'd be far more subtle about it.

**Rosanna**   He's banking on you thinking that.

**Deanne**   Credit where it's due he's good.

**Katie**   What?

**Deanne**   He's a fucking genius.

**Rosanna**   Left his phone here.

**Deanne**   Nice touch.

**Rosanna**   Made us think we wanted ice when all along it was just a cunning ploy to get out the house.

**Deanne**   Impressive.

**Rosanna**   Ooh I do like that Dermot O'Leary.

**Deanne**   I thought you didn't want a younger man?

**Rosanna**   I could make an exception.

**Rosanna** *and* **Deanne** *crack up.*

**Katie**    Before Bubba was born how many kids did we have between us?

**Rosanna**    Huh?

**Katie**    You heard.

**Rosanna**    I don't know.

**Deanne**    Seven.

**Katie**    Seven.

**Rosanna**    So what?

**Katie**    How many fathers between them?

**Deanne**    Six.

**Katie**    That's right.

**Rosanna**    So what?

**Katie**    And not one of them present. Not one.

**Rosanna**    Four of those fathers are Deanne's. She has more babyfathers than I have pairs of pants.

**Katie**    Frank's here.

**Rosanna**    Here is he?

**Rosanna** *looks at an imaginary* **Frank**.

Oh hello Frank nice to see you.

**Katie**    He'll be here.

**Rosanna**    He'll be high as a kite.

**Katie**    He doesn't do that. That's why he's here.

**Rosanna**    We'll see.

**Katie**    Add Kelly's two and that's nine kids on this street alone nine kids without their father. And this is a cul-de-sac. Imagine if we lived on the High Road.

**Deanne**    What's happened with Kelly?

**Rosanna**   Haven't you heard?

**Deanne**   No.

**Rosanna**   Pete's gone and left her.

**Deanne**   No?

**Katie**   Not so much left her as told her to leave. With the kids.

**Deanne**   He's done what?

**Katie**   The house is his. She has no rights. They're not married.

**Deanne**   He can't kick her out?

**Rosanna**   He has. And all because she told him it was over. All because she caught him having an affair. The dirty dog. I've a good mind to go down there myself. Tell him a few things.

**Deanne**   Stay out of it you.

**Rosanna**   Why?

**Deanne**   It's none of your business.

**Rosanna**   She needs support. A friend in need is a friend . . .

**Rosanna** *can't find the end of the saying*.

**Deanne**   How awful.

**Rosanna**   He pissed on her.

**Deanne**   What?

**Rosanna**   He came home last night drunk. She starts shouting at him. He pisses on her.

**Deanne**   Pisses on her?

**Rosanna**   Pisses on her. What bit of that don't you understand? Have you ever heard the word piss? Well he. Pissed. On her.

**Deanne**   He pissed on her?

**Rosanna**   Whatever gave you that idea?

**Deanne**   Are you serious?

**Rosanna**   No I'm joking. Yes he pissed on her. I don't know how to make it any more plain. Urinated. There is that better?

**Deanne**   I can't believe it.

**Rosanna**   You better believe it.

**Deanne**   Shocking.

**Rosanna**   And she's got the nerve to look down on me.

**Katie**   She doesn't.

**Rosanna**   All because I send my kids to state school.

**Katie**   What?

**Rosanna**   Because her kids have a golden fanny and a golden dick they have to go private.

**Katie**   Are you serious?

**Rosanna**   Who does her cleaning?

**Deanne**   Who?

**Rosanna**   Not you.

**Deanne**   No of course I don't do it I have my own cleaning.

**Rosanna**   Did you hear that? She does her own cleaning.

**Katie**   Are you having a pop at me?

**Rosanna**   I'm just saying.

**Katie**   As if I haven't got enough on my plate I have to do my own cleaning?

**Rosanna**   You work. You have a baby. You have a right to have a cleaner. What does *she* do?

**Katie**   It's difficult in her position.

**Rosanna**    Sounds cushty to me.

**Katie**    Pete's undermined her confidence. She's been very brave telling him to leave. Even if that means *she* has to leave. She depends on him for money. He won't give her anything now. He's said as much.

**Rosanna**    She can *work*.

**Katie**    Not so easy when you've been cooped up at home so long.

**Rosanna**    My heart bleeds. How can she complain when her kids go private. When she *chooses* not to work. When she has a cleaner. *I* don't have that luxury. I'm sorry.

**Katie**    This has nothing to do with private school. What the *fuck* are you talking about? Her fella's an alcoholic. He's destroying his life. He's taking her and her children down with him through no fault of her own.

**Rosanna**    So she deserves compassion but I don't?

**Katie**    I never said that.

**Rosanna**    Have you told *her* to go to meetings?

**Katie**    Plenty of times.

**Rosanna**    And?

**Katie**    She won't go.

**Rosanna**    Good for her.

**Katie**    Quite the opposite in fact. If she went to meetings she'd have support. She'd have some understanding. Some acceptance. Some tools to help her cope. She might be able to rebuild her life.

**Rosanna**    Shall we have a whip-round?

**Katie**    What?

**Rosanna**    We'll have one for Jim and one for Kelly. How about that? That way she can have a butler as well as a cleaner. She can have psychotherapy. Meanwhile my kids have to *work* over the holidays. I don't see *her* kids working.

**Katie**   They're six and ten.

**Rosanna** *looks nonplussed.*

**Rosanna**   Too soft you.

**Katie**   Too hard you.

**Rosanna**   Whatever.

*They all gaze at the telly.*

**Katie**   That's awful news Dee.

**Deanne**   I'm cut up.

**Katie**   I bet you are.

**Deanne**   I don't know how I'm going to cope.

**Rosanna**   It's cos he's Jamaican.

**Katie**   What?

**Rosanna**   Predisposed.

**Katie**   You reckon?

**Deanne**   I know so.

**Rosanna**   Fat. Black. Likes a drink. Textbook.

**Deanne**   How's he ever going to remember to take his medication. That's why I told him, the party's over son, a new way of life.

**Katie**   He's got a family it's about time.

**Rosanna**   Innit.

**Deanne**   My beautiful baby boy.

**Katie**   I'm sorry Deanne.

**Rosanna**   You see Kate?

**Katie**   What?

**Rosanna**   My Jack's ill. Her Reggie. And all you can do is go on about the plight of your fella. Your ex. *My* ex. Three men living the life of Riley by the look of it. I don't see *them* having to take insulin. Having tubes coming out of their body. My son and his father are both pumped up to the eyeballs on drugs, only difference is, one has no say in the matter and the other . . .

**Katie**   Has no say in the matter.

**Rosanna** *smirks.*

**Rosanna**   Please.

**Katie** *gets up, puts her plate and fork by the sink, and starts making herself a mug of tea.*

**Katie**   If everytime you took drugs you ended up in a state of terror would you take them? If there was no fun involved at all only pain. If you ended up all alone and destitute. Your life broken. You. Everyone. Everything. Broken. In a closet the door bolted the phone on nine nine nine. Everytime. No exceptions. If you couldn't put one in your system without going on a binge and you knew the consequences as the consequences were always the same but you still couldn't stop yourself from doing it. If you lost your home. Everyone you loved. If you burned every bridge you'd ever built both professionally and personally. Would you still take drugs? If drugs nearly cost you your life if you'd come fifteen minutes from death if you'd turned up at the hospital fifteen minutes later you'd be dead. If you found yourself in a hospital bed with 'tubes' coming out of your body. Would you take them? Cos that's what happened to Frank.

**Deanne**   That happened to Frank?

**Katie**   And more. Everything he's ever had. Broken. Destroyed. Opportunity. Sabotaged. Anyone who's ever shown any interest in him. Any belief. Any love. He couldn't be loved he didn't know how to accept love he didn't love himself. He didn't let anything touch him that's why he medicated himself. He didn't want to feel. He was incapable of being with himself so deep were his feelings of self-loathing. Before drugs it was food and before that it was self-harming. From a young age. Mutilated himself. Why? Because it took him away from himself. However much harm he caused himself it felt better than the pain he was in already. Not that he knew anything about it.

**Deanne**    What do you mean?

**Katie**    He kept it a secret not only from others but also from himself.

**Deanne**    From himself?

**Katie**    He was in denial.

**Deanne**    How can you be in denial about that?

**Rosanna**    You've got the scars all over your body for fuck sake.

**Katie**    You'd be surprised what we can keep from ourselves. We're often the last person to know. Denial is a staggering thing.

**Deanne**    Imagine abusing yourself and not even realising.

**Katie**    Imagine Deanne.

**Deanne**    Incredible.

**Katie**    Incredible.

**Deanne**    No I don't believe it.

**Katie**    It's true.

**Deanne**    But that's impossible.

**Katie**    It is not.

**Deanne**    You've got to be totally fucking deluded.

**Katie**    Fraid so.

**Deanne**    Well I never.

**Katie**    Every decision he made. Bad. Every action he took. Bad. Bad for those around him bad for himself. Bad. Just bad. If a sign said this way for a healthy and fruitful life, he went the other way. If a sign said this way for a life of misery and despair, he took it. Perhaps unwittingly but he took it. Without fail. Drawn to the gutter through forces beyond his control. Would you say that's normal behaviour or would you say you're suffering from something?

**Rosanna**    I'd say you were mad.

**Katie**    And if you were mad would it be your fault? Is that what we do? Go around blaming mad people for being mad?

**Rosanna**    I'm not disputing he can't stop. Or couldn't stop. I'm just saying you can't compare it to an illness. My Jack's ill. Ill forever.

**Katie**    It's alcohol*ism* not alcohol*wasm*. You can't be cured of it you can only recover. But you're only one drink away from death. *Forever*.

**Rosanna**    Frank made a choice.

**Katie**    He did not.

**Rosanna**    I'm not saying he couldn't stop. How many times do I have to repeat it? I'm saying at some point in his life he made a choice. There was a line and he crossed it and he *chose* to cross it and once he went over that line – granted – he was too far away from the shore to swim back. I know when it happened to Jimmy. It was when his mum died. Then his brother. That's when everything changed. That's when he chose to blot it out. Up til then he'd only been recreational. Then it got serious. If he'd have been braver or stronger he'd have toughed it out. Communicated with me. Sought help through other means instead of acting so damn selfishly.

**Katie**    What about all those other addicts whose mothers haven't died?

**Rosanna**    Then something else happened to them.

**Katie**   What about those who come from perfectly happy homes? No trauma. No nothing.

**Rosanna**   Something triggered it. Somewhere along the line they made a choice. I'm sorry if their choice backfired. That's not my fault.

**Katie**   They used to say the same about gays.

**Rosanna**   What?

**Katie**   They used to say *that* was a choice. You were punished for it. Victimised. Strangely enough the people who all said that were straight. What are the chances? They were experts on being gay. Go figure.

**Rosanna** *looks nonplussed*.

**Rosanna**   Here Dee do you want to go speed dating?

**Deanne**   What?

**Rosanna**   Me and you.

**Deanne**   Speed dating?

**Rosanna**   There's plenty of places. I've looked into it.

**Deanne**   Nah I can't.

**Rosanna**   Why not?

**Deanne**   I don't have enough confidence.

**Rosanna**   What do you mean you're a man-eater.

**Deanne**   I need to lose some weight. Perhaps next summer.

**Rosanna**   I can't wait til then.

**Deanne**   I'm going on a diet. I'm cutting out the booze. Once and for all.

**Katie**   Do you think you can?

**Deanne**   Of course I can.

**Katie**   Do you ever think you might have a problem?

**Deanne**   What?

**Katie**   Uh-hu.

**Deanne**   Are you kidding?

**Katie**   No.

**Deanne** *looks nonplussed.*

**Deanne**   Did you hear that? She thinks I've got a problem with drink.

**Deanne** *bursts into laughter.*

**Katie**   Then stop.

**Deanne**   Why should I?

**Katie**   You're always talking about it.

**Deanne**   Next summer.

**Katie**   What about now?

**Deanne**   During The X Factor? Are you mad? We're down to the last eight. This is no time to stop.

**Rosanna**   How can she stop now we're down to the last eight.

**Deanne**   Exactly.

**Rosanna**   Give a girl a break.

**Deanne**   Exactly.

**Rosanna**   Wait til the series has finished at least.

**Deanne**   Exactly.

**Rosanna**   Then she can stop.

**Deanne**   I've always said I'll stop just as soon as The X Factor stops. The X Factor stops *I* stop that's the deal.

**Rosanna**   You said that last series.

**Deanne**   I wasn't ready. This time I'm ready. Last year was too good. How could you stop drinking after that? This year ain't nearly the same. The acts are shit and that Dannii Minogue? Well, let's not go into it.

**Katie**   What's wrong with her?

**Rosanna**'s *face drops.*

**Rosanna**   What's wrong with her?

**Deanne**   Have you been watching?

**Katie**   Funnily enough I've had trouble concentrating.

**Deanne**   She's shit.

**Rosanna**   She's more than shit she's a disgrace to womankind.

**Katie**   Why is she?

**Rosanna**   All that plastic.

**Katie**   She's ill.

**Rosanna**'s *face drops.*

**Rosanna**   She's what?

**Katie**   I feel sorry for her.

**Deanne**   All I know is she's bloody awful. The only reason she got that job is cos Simon Cowell fancies her.

**Rosanna**   There you go you see. What did I tell you? Does he want a real woman or does he want a Barbie doll? What sort of message does that send the kids?

**Katie**   I'm not disputing that.

**Rosanna**   Well then.

**Katie**   All I'm saying is she's probably in a dark place.

**Rosanna** *groans.*

**Rosanna**   Oh here we go.

**Katie**   Altering herself like that. And so regularly. She hardly strikes me as someone with a high self-regard.

**Rosanna**    Look at her she can hardly move.

**Katie**    Exactly.

**Rosanna**    Everytime she looks sideways she has to turn her whole body.

**Deanne**    She's like a robot.

**Rosanna**    R2-D2.

**Rosanna** and **Deanne** *crack up*.

**Katie**    She's been hired for that very reason. Can't you see that? Everyone wants to gawp at her. She fulfils a fantasy in men and she arouses curiosity in women.

**Rosanna**    Loathing more like.

**Katie**    She's a victim.

**Rosanna**    She's successful.

**Katie**    No amount of external factors can fix what's going on inside.

**Rosanna**    Is that right?

**Katie**    Lippo, botox, implants.

**Rosanna**    And the rest.

**Deanne**    Look at her.

**Katie**    It doesn't fill the gaping hole inside.

**Rosanna**    That gaping hole inside has been caused by having all the fat sucked out of her body. *That's* the gaping hole.

**Katie**    There's no chemical solution to a spiritual problem.

**Rosanna**    Is that right?

**Katie**    It is. She's probably as miserable as sin.

**Rosanna**    Then the cheques come in and she suddenly becomes happy.

**Deanne**    What are the chances?

**Katie**    It's an inside job.

**Rosanna**    You don't half talk some crap. She's living the life of Riley.

**Katie**    She's unhappy.

**Rosanna**    Know her well?

**Katie**    It's etched all over her face.

**Rosanna**    *Nothing's* etched all over her face. That's why she had botox.

**Rosanna** *and* **Deanne** *crack up.*

**Katie**    Have it your way. I know you think a man's the answer to all your woes. Sorry to suggest doing some work on yourself.

**Deanne**    I tell you what, that Simon Cowell could certainly solve a few of *my* woes. Let me tell you that now.

**Deanne** *leers at the telly.*

**Katie**    You fancy him?

**Deanne**    Who wouldn't?

**Rosanna**    Are you sure?

**Deanne**    He's always right Katie. Everything he says. Right. What woman wouldn't want to be with him? If he's always right, and he wants you to be his woman, what does that say about you?

**Rosanna**    That you're a Barbie doll with no personality.

**Deanne** *shakes her head.*

**Deanne**    Exercise is key. That's the key to it. Forget your botox. If you exercise you can eat what you want. Botox just smoothens the skin. Wear a mask. Botox won't help you fit into a nice sexy number. Figure-hugging. Showing off your best assets.

**Rosanna** *roars her approval.*

I'll be down that gym every day. You watch. And I'm getting extensions. Basically I'm going to look like Mariah Carey.

**Deanne** *looks pleased with herself.*

**Katie**    Mariah Carey?

**Rosanna**    She's had more plastic than any of them.

**Deanne**    Do you think I wouldn't have it if I could afford it? A tummy tuck? Of *course* I would. Do you think I want to stop the booze and do exercise? You're mad. What sort of ridiculous idea is that? Are you two off your head? I've got better things to do with my time. I'm a busy woman I've got a life. What happened to the curry?

**Deanne** *has finished the remainder of the takeaway including what was left on* **Katie**'s *plate.*

Fuck that.

**Deanne** *finishes her drink.*

Who *are* these shysters?

**Deanne** *looks at the name of the curry house on the menu.*

**Rosanna**    Sit down.

**Deanne**    I *will* sit down. I need a *lie* down after all that food. I feel a bit queasy.

**Rosanna**    Have a drink.

**Deanne**    I *will* have a drink. Let me just sit down first. Everything in moderation. Let's just take it 'nice and easy'.

**Katie** *sits down on the sofa with her tea.* **Deanne** *leaves her glass in the kitchen and plumps herself between* **Katie** *and* **Rosanna**, *nearly crushing them, causing* **Katie**'s *tea to spill.*

**Katie**    Oi.

**Rosanna**    Do you mind?

**Deanne**    Get that fucking food away from me.

**Deanne** *looks like she's going to retch.*

Seriously.

**Katie** *pushes* **Frank**'s *plate further away from* **Deanne**.

**Katie**    Fucking hell.

**Deanne**    You should watch what you're doing.

**Katie** *sighs and gets up.*

Oh that's right blame me. Pick on Deanne is that what we're going to play.

**Deanne** *nods.*

Fine.

**Katie** *puts her mug by the sink, gets a cloth, cleans herself, and starts cleaning up the spilt tea.*

Katie I didn't mean it.

**Katie**    I know.

**Deanne**    I didn't mean it.

**Katie**    I know.

**Deanne**    Accident.

**Katie**    It's okay.

**Deanne**    I love you.

**Katie**    I love you too.

**Deanne**    No hard feelings.

**Katie**    Will you shut up.

**Deanne**    Temper temper. Chill out. No-one's died. Fucking hell. Blimey.

**Deanne** *looks affronted.*

Fuck me.

**Katie** *puts the cloth by the sink and dries her hands with a tea towel.*

**Katie**   Do you want some water?

**Deanne**   Excuse me?

**Katie**   Ignore me.

**Deanne**   I think I will.

**Deanne** *plumps up the vacant cushion beside her.*

Here make yourself comfy. Perch yourself on that pew. Take the weight off your feet. Take your mind off things. We all have our own problems. Not just you. Christ don't be so self-obsessed.

**Katie** *sits back down on the sofa.*

That's it sit down you're getting right on my wick.

*Someone is heard entering the building downstairs.*

**Rosanna**   That's Frank.

**Katie**   What?

**Rosanna**   That's him downstairs.

**Deanne**   Aye aye. This will be interesting.

**Deanne** *tries her best to straighten herself and make herself presentable.*

Probably off his head the dirty scoundrel.

*They all stare at the front door.*

**Part Two**

*As you were. The kitchen tops are strewn with empty takeaway*
*cartons and dirty spoons, two dirty plates and dirty forks, two empty*
*glasses, a mug, a used tea bag, a tea towel, a cloth, a bottle of rum*
*and a bottle of coke, apple juice and milk.* **Frank**'s *plate of food*
*and* **Rosanna**'s *rum and coke remain untouched on the coffee table.*
**Deanne** *is sitting between* **Katie** *and* **Rosanna** *on the sofa. They*
*are all staring at* **Frank** *who is standing just inside the front*
*doorway. He looks nonplussed.*

**Frank**    What's up?

**Katie**    Where you been?

**Frank**    Next door. Sorry I was so long.

**Katie**    What you been doing?

**Frank**    Playing video games.

**Katie**    Your food's cold.

**Frank**    I'll heat it up.

**Katie**    Playing video games you don't play video games.

**Frank**    I was a dab hand when I was young. The boys
challenged me.

**Frank** *gestures like he had no choice but to take up the challenge.*

**Katie**    Where's the ice?

**Frank** *looks nonplussed.*

**Frank**    You what?

**Katie**    The ice.

**Frank**    I knew there was something I forgot.

**Rosanna**    He forgot the ice.

**Frank**    I'll just go and get it.

**Katie**    Don't go anywhere.

**Frank**   I'll only be a minute.

**Katie**   You said that before remember?

**Frank**   What's eating you guys? If you wanted ice so badly you could always have come down and got it.

**Rosanna**   Clever.

**Frank**   What is?

**Rosanna**   Doff your cap Deanne.

**Deanne**   Will someone pass me the sick bag.

**Frank**   What's up with her?

**Rosanna**   Bit too much food.

**Katie**   Didn't want to see it go to waste.

**Frank**   Look. I forgot the ice. I got a bit caught up with the boys. Am I pardoned?

**Katie**   No you're not pardoned. You've been gone the best part of an hour.

**Frank**   Have not.

**Katie**   Have so.

**Frank**   An *hour*?

**Rosanna**   An hour.

**Frank**   My God doesn't time fly. I don't know what came over me. They're very addictive those things.

**Katie**   You didn't take your phone.

**Frank** *looks nonplussed.*

**Frank**   What?

**Katie**   You heard.

**Frank**   I thought I was going down for two minutes.

**Katie**   I trusted you.

**Frank**    What are you on about?

**Katie** *doesn't answer.*

Call them.

**Katie**    No.

**Frank**    Go on. Call them. They'll soon put your mind at rest.

**Katie**    No.

**Frank**    Why not?

**Katie**    It's fine.

**Frank**    Call them.

**Katie**    I don't want to.

**Frank**    *I'll* call them.

**Katie**    No. It's fine.

**Frank**    I'll call them.

**Frank** *collects his phone and starts scrolling.*

**Katie**    Don't you dare.

**Frank**    What?

**Frank** *stops scrolling.*

**Rosanna**    No let him call them Kate.

**Katie**    Put it down.

**Rosanna**    Then we can put all this to bed.

**Katie**    Where it was.

**Frank**    Oh for fuck sake.

**Katie**    Just there.

**Frank**    Don't say I didn't offer.

**Frank** *holds out his phone.*

It's a good offer Kate.

**Frank** *holds out his phone.*

One of the best.

**Katie**    Down.

**Frank** *puts down his phone.*

**Rosanna**    Honestly I give up.

**Frank**    This ain't about me Katie.

**Rosanna** *scoffs.*

This is about you. This is about Zane and Minny.

**Rosanna**    Who's Minny?

**Frank** *doesn't answer.*

**Katie**    Minny's Zane's new wife.

**Rosanna**    He got married?

**Deanne**    When was this?

**Katie**    You piped up.

**Frank**    They got married last week in Las Vegas.

**Rosanna**    Did Chrissie go?

**Frank**    Chrissie wasn't invited. It was all hush-hush.

**Katie**    Off the cuff.

**Rosanna**    How long have they been going out?

**Frank**    Three weeks.

**Rosanna**    Three weeks?

**Katie**    What do you want he's a rock n roll star.

**Rosanna**    Where's she from?

**Deanne**    Who is she?

**Rosanna**    How did they meet?

**Katie**    They met in rehab.

**Rosanna**   I might have known.

**Frank**   She's younger than him.

**Rosanna**   How much younger?

**Katie**   Substantially.

**Rosanna**   How much?

**Frank**   She's a baby.

**Katie**   Early twenties.

**Rosanna**   Have you met her?

**Katie**   I've met her and she's nice. Bit manic. Well-meaning.

**Rosanna**   What was her vice?

**Katie**   Heroin.

**Rosanna**   Heroin?

**Katie**   She's off that now.

**Rosanna**   So she's cleaned up her act?

**Katie**   Sort of. They do the odd bit of spliff.

**Frank**   And drink.

**Katie**   And coke.

**Rosanna**   Straight out of rehab?

**Katie** *nods*.

It won't last.

**Katie**   I know.

**Rosanna**   And Chrissie's there?

**Katie**   She's with her dad Saturdays. She loves being with her dad. She loves Minny.

**Rosanna**   I'm not surprised. They're almost the same age.

**Katie**   That's uncalled for.

**Rosanna**  Is she beautiful?

**Katie**  She's pretty.

**Deanne**  Skinny?

**Frank**  Very.

**Katie**  She has an eating disorder.

**Rosanna**  Oh bloody hell I've heard it all.

**Deanne**  We have to get Chrissie away from there.

**Katie**  We do not.

**Frank**  She's safe with her dad.

**Rosanna**  How do you know?

**Frank**  They might use but they wouldn't use when she's around.

**Rosanna**  Know this for a fact do you?

**Katie**  Yes.

**Rosanna**  Who knows what's going on there.

**Katie**  Nothing's going on there. Minny's very good with kids. She loves kids.

**Frank**  She has kids.

**Rosanna**  She *has* kids?

**Katie** *doesn't answer.*

How many?

**Katie**  Two.

**Rosanna**  *Two?*

**Katie** *doesn't answer.*

Where are they?

**Katie**  With their dad.

**Rosanna**    They go to their dad's on Saturdays?

**Katie**    They're with their dad.

**Frank**    Full stop.

**Katie**    She doesn't have custody.

**Rosanna**    Bloody hell Kate.

**Katie**    I know.

**Rosanna**    Have you spoken to her?

**Katie**    Who?

**Rosanna**    Chrissie.

**Katie**    Since when?

**Rosanna**    Since you dropped her off.

**Katie**    No.

**Rosanna**    Perhaps you should.

**Katie**    If she knows that I'm worried *she'll* be worried. These things transmit themselves. I can't be checking up on her every two minutes. We speak before she goes to bed. That's ample.

**Rosanna**    No wonder you're a bag of nerves.

**Katie**    I am not.

**Rosanna**    No wonder you're taking it out on Frankie.

**Deanne**    Poor Frankie.

**Rosanna** *waves* **Frank** *towards her.*

**Rosanna**    Come here sit down.

**Deanne** *waves* **Frank** *towards her.*

**Deanne**    Take the weight off your feet.

**Deanne** *budges up, squashing* **Katie**.

Budge up.

**Katie** *is forced to get up, sitting down on the armchair instead.*

**Rosanna**    Take your shoes off.

**Rosanna** *and* **Deanne** *make* **Frank** *sit down between them.*

**Deanne**    Here let me do it.

**Deanne** *helps* **Frank** *slip out of his shoes.*

**Rosanna**    Katie thought you were on drugs I told her not to worry.

**Deanne**    She thought you'd been seeing my Victor.

**Rosanna**    She had it all worked out.

**Katie**    Don't be stupid.

**Deanne**    Drug test.

**Rosanna**    What?

**Deanne**    Strip search.

*The others look nonplussed.*

You hold him while I pull his kecks off.

**Deanne** *starts trying to undo* **Frank**'s *trousers and pull them off.*

**Frank**    Oi hold up.

**Frank** *starts fending her off.*

**Deanne**    Come here.

**Frank**    Do you *mind*?

**Rosanna**    What on *earth* are you doing?

**Deanne**    He's hiding them in *there* the crafty bugger.

**Frank**    I am *not*.

**Deanne**    Look at that bulge don't tell me you haven't got them in there.

**Frank** *resists as* **Deanne** *tries to grab his crotch.*

**Frank**   I have *not*.

**Deanne**   You've got a packet in your packet no *wonder* it's so big.

**Frank**   Leave my packet *alone*.

**Katie**   *Deanne.*

**Rosanna**   Get a grip of yourself.

**Deanne**   Oh sorry.

**Deanne** *suddenly comes to her senses.*

**Frank**   I should think so.

**Deanne**   I don't know what came over me.

**Rosanna**   'Eeeaasy tiger'.

**Rosanna** *cracks up.*

Let's just take it 'nice and easy' hey? Dear oh dear.

**Rosanna** *cracks up.*

Have a drink.

**Deanne**   I *will* have a drink. How can I have a drink without ice? I tell you what *I'll* get the ice. Don't you worry your pretty little head.

**Deanne** *strokes* **Frank**'s *head.*

Oops I can't get up.

**Deanne** *tries to get up but can't.*

I told you this would happen. Remember? I told you I was stuck here. Rum and apple. I'm still in a state of shock. What happens if I need to go to the toilet?

**Rosanna**   Here Frank get her a bedpan.

**Rosanna** *and* **Deanne** *crack up.*

**Deanne**   Make that a *large* one.

**Rosanna** *and* **Deanne** *crack up.*

**Rosanna**    Ooh this is the life.

**Frank** *and* **Katie** *look at each other as if to say 'what's got into these guys?'.*

**Deanne**    Fetch the ice I can't have a drink without ice. What sort of person do you take me for? I like a drink but only under the right conditions. I won't drink just willy-nilly. Everything has to be right. I have to have a glass for example. I won't drink out of the bottle. That's what pigs do. I like my drink chilled. If it's not chilled I'll wait. I'll wait for it to be chilled. I want ice. I want a slice. I want someone to talk to. I don't want to drink and not talk to anybody. I want to have a nice time. I like to mix it I won't drink it straight. That's what pigs do. I want some soda water. I want some ginger ale. I don't want apple juice Frank. That's what pigs do. I want something proper. Something that goes with what I'm drinking. Otherwise I won't drink it.

**Rosanna**    *I'll* get the ice.

**Deanne**    You do that.

**Rosanna**    Watch and learn Frank.

**Deanne**    Show him will you.

**Rosanna**    I will.

**Deanne**    You do that.

**Rosanna**    If a job needs doing it needs doing properly.

**Deanne**    That's what *I* always say.

**Rosanna**    The secret to getting ice is getting ice. Not pretending to get it. Actually getting it. Gordon Ramsay should do a series on it. Gordon Ramsay's Guide To Getting Ice.

**Deanne**    Brilliant

**Rosanna** *and* **Deanne** *crack up.*

Off we trot.

**Rosanna** *reaches for her shoes*.

**Deanne**    Don't get caught playing video games.

**Rosanna**    As if.

**Deanne**    You know what they're like.

**Frank**    They're quite persuasive.

**Rosanna**    Maybe to you perhaps not to me. No way could Danny ever persuade me to join in with him.

**Deanne**    He does play a lot.

**Rosanna**    He loves those games.

**Katie**    Maybe too much.

**Rosanna**    What do you mean?

**Katie**    What was his trigger Rose?

**Frank**    Hey?

**Rosanna**    What do you mean?

**Katie**    I thought you needed a 'trigger'?

**Rosanna**    He's not addicted.

**Katie**    Oh no?

**Rosanna**    Are you taking the piss?

**Deanne**    Like father like son.

**Rosanna**    He's nothing *like* his father.

**Katie**    He's always on that couch playing those things.

**Rosanna**    Where would you rather he were? Would you rather he were hanging out on street corners? Would you rather I didn't know his whereabouts? There's a lot worse places he could be.

**Katie**    Doubtless.

**Rosanna**    Well then.

**Katie**    He's a good boy.

**Deanne**    He's a lovely boy.

**Rosanna**    Well then shut up.

**Frank**    What about your daughter?

**Katie**    What do you mean?

**Frank**    Chrissie.

**Katie**    Yes I know her name.

**Frank**    Don't be angry.

**Katie**    I'm not angry.

**Rosanna**    Yes you are look at you.

**Frank**    Spends all day on the internet.

**Katie**    She does not.

**Frank** *looks at* **Katie** *as if to say 'really?'.*

I'll have to ration her.

**Frank**    You've been saying that for ages.

**Katie**    She has a very obsessional nature.

**Rosanna**    Obsessional is it?

**Katie**    You've seen what she's like with teddy bears.

**Deanne**    Teddy bears?

**Frank**    She has about a million. If you ask her what she wants she says another teddy bear. No sooner does she get another than she wants another. Have you seen downstairs?

**Deanne**    No.

**Frank**    You can't move for them.

**Rosanna**    She's eleven years old.

**Frank**   She likes teddy bears.

**Katie**   What can you do?

**Rosanna**   I reckon you can drag her away from the internet. Don't ask. *Tell*.

**Katie**   The way you tell your Danny?

**Rosanna**   He's fine.

**Katie**   His schoolwork suffers.

**Rosanna**   It does not.

**Deanne**   His grades.

**Rosanna**   We've been through that.

**Deanne**   Have we?

**Rosanna**   Yes we have. He's not an academic.

**Katie**   He spends all day on that settee.

**Rosanna**   He does not.

**Deanne**   Of course he does.

**Rosanna**   Will you lay off him?

**Frank**   He dawdles.

**Rosanna**   So what?

**Frank**   Daydreams.

**Rosanna**   And?

**Frank**   I'm just saying.

**Rosanna**   *What* exactly?

**Frank**   Listen Rose don't take this the wrong way. I like your Danny. I identify with him.

**Katie**   Frank loves Danny. He's always saying.

**Rosanna**   Loves him? He hasn't got a good word to *say* about him.

**Katie**    That's not true.

**Rosanna**    I don't have to sit here and take this.

**Frank**    I'm sorry I mentioned it.

**Rosanna**    My Danny's a good boy.

**Frank**    Undoubtedly.

**Rosanna**    You really think . . . ?

**Frank**    I didn't say that.

**Rosanna**    Right that's it. I'm going to go down and tell him. No more video games. It's Saturday night he should be out partying.

**Deanne**    He doesn't want to.

**Rosanna**    No he'd far rather stay in with Spark. Doing what? They don't even say two words to each other. They grunt.

**Frank**    Don't worry unduly.

**Rosanna**    What do you mean? You identify with him. You said so yourself.

**Frank**    It doesn't mean anything.

**Rosanna** *gets up.*

**Rosanna**    I'm going to put a stop to all this. Sort it out once and for all. He's not going to end up like you. No way. I'd rather he was an Al-Qaeda terrorist. No offence.

**Katie**    Don't be hard on him.

**Rosanna** *scoffs.*

**Deanne**    Don't forget the ice.

**Rosanna** *stomps off through the front door.* **Deanne** *shouts after her.*

Remember Gordon Ramsay.

**Frank**    She's going to go apeshit.

**Katie**    It's not your fault.

**Frank**   She's scared shitless.

**Deanne**   Not as scared as *he's* going to be.

**Katie** *and* **Deanne** *laugh.*

**Frank**   Listen Kate I'm sorry about that.

**Deanne**   About what?

**Frank**   What I said.

**Deanne**   What did you say?

**Frank**   About Minny. I shouldn't have divulged your business.

**Deanne**   It's alright.

**Frank**   It's not alright. I was wrong. I was getting back at you. It was uncalled for. You had a right to be worried about me and I should have shut my gob. I'm sorry.

**Katie**   It's okay. You weren't too wide of the mark. I am worried.

**Frank**   I know you are but it's private.

**Katie**   It's done now.

**Deanne**   Did they really get married in Las Vegas?

**Katie** *nods.*

Fantastic.

**Katie**   If you say so.

**Deanne**   She's a lucky lass.

**Katie**   If you say so.

**Deanne**   Fuck me what I wouldn't do to marry a rock star.

**Frank**   Go to rehab. They're all in there.

**Deanne**   Maybe I *should* go to rehab. Do you think they'd employ me?

**Katie**   I don't think they'd ever let you go.

**Deanne**  Ahh that's nice.

**Deanne** *has misunderstood* **Katie** *and beams with pride.*

You say the nicest things. That's why I love you Katie. You really are a cuddly little monkey. I want to tickle you. Let me tickle you.

**Katie**  No.

**Katie** *and* **Deanne** *laugh.*

**Deanne**  Oh go on.

**Katie**  No.

**Deanne**  Get the booze out.

**Katie**  What?

**Deanne**  The secret bottle.

**Katie**  What secret bottle?

**Deanne**  The one you're hiding from Rosie.

**Katie**  I'm not hiding anything from her.

**Deanne**  Oh come on. You know what she's like. *I'd* hide my booze from her too if I were you. You're safe now.

**Katie**  There's no bottle.

**Deanne**  That's all you got?

**Katie**  That's it.

**Deanne**  Nothing stashed away?

**Katie**  Fraid not.

**Deanne**  Blimey. I was convinced you were stashing something away for later.

**Katie**  No.

**Deanne**  That's it?

**Frank**  That's it.

**Deanne**   Not very good is it?

**Frank**   Sorry.

**Deanne**   I should think so. Do you know what *I've* got at home?

**Frank**   What?

**Deanne**   I've got it all. Anything you want I got it. You want Stella or Becks I got both. You can have Stella *or* Becks it's up to you. If you want a Stella you can have Stella. If you want Becks you can have that. I don't care. It's all the same to me.

**Frank**   Have you got anything besides Becks or Stella?

**Deanne** *looks nonplussed.*

**Deanne**   Are you taking the piss?

**Frank**   No.

**Deanne**   I've got loads more. I've got vodka wine gin. I've got schnaps. Have *you* got schnaps?

**Frank**   No.

**Deanne**   Well then. Isn't it about time you got schnaps?

**Frank**   I don't have much call for it.

**Deanne**   Always be prepared. That's my motto. You never know when the situation might arise. You'd think you don't need schnaps you could be happily toddling along when one day the situation arises and presto, it's there. That's what I call forward thinking. I don't like to get caught with my knickers down.

**Frank**   Evidently.

**Deanne**   Mind you the shops are still open I suppose. No stress. Stress not Katie the shops are still open.

**Katie**   I know they are.

**Deanne**   I'm just saying. You looked a bit scared there for a minute. It's fine. Panic over.

*They all gaze at the telly.*

Let's just all chill out.

*They all gaze at the telly.*

Everyone's getting a little bit over-excited.

*A text alert goes.*

Oh hello.

*They all check their phone.*

Rosanna.

**Rosanna**'s *left her phone in the flat.*

Shall we read it?

**Katie** *and* **Deanne** *laugh.*

Oh go on Kate please.

**Katie** *and* **Deanne** *laugh.*

I wonder who it is?

*They all gaze at the telly.*

Who could be texting her at this time?

**Katie**    It's not late.

**Deanne**    I never said it was. Don't jump down my throat.

**Katie**    I'm not.

**Katie** *looks nonplussed while* **Deanne** *looks affronted.*

**Frank**    You should have seen me Kate. Those boys don't know what hit them. Form is temporary but class is permanent. I'm a dab hand.

**Katie**    You beat them?

**Frank**    It was a massacre. It was embarrassing. Really. Even *I* was embarrassed for them. Do you know how much time they spend on those things? And then I walk in and blow them out of the water. I walk in, I sit down, I get to work. I don't talk I do. I'm a doer Katie.

**Katie**    Yeah right.

**Frank**    They weren't expecting it. You should have seen the look on their faces it was beautiful. Priceless. You should have been there. It was one of those glorious moments in life. It'll be forever etched in there. You're not going to erase this memory in a long time. In a very long time. This was a victory. Not just for me but for all of us.

**Katie**    How do you work that out?

**Frank**    Kids. Those kids need to be shown a thing or two. They've no respect. I showed them. I taught them who was running this show and it's not them. It's me. I'm the boss around here. 'I'm running tings'. Next time they see me they'll see me in a new light. They'll shut up. They'll shut up. Don't tell me that's not a victory. That's a victory.

**Katie**    No wonder you were gone so long.

**Frank**    Exactly. You see. I was teaching them a thing or two. I was putting them in their place. I was doing it for the good of society Kate not just me. I was thinking of all the kids out there who terrorise their elders. I was thinking of them. I was doing what they wanted to do only they don't have the dexterity. They don't have the nimbleness in their fingers. They don't have the technique. Well I've got it and I showed it.

**Katie**    Good.

**Frank**    Not good Kate. 'Great'.

**Katie**    Great.

**Frank**    'Phenomenal'.

**Katie**    I'm pleased for you.

**Frank**    Don't be pleased for me. Be pleased for the world. It's the world that benefits, not me.

**Katie**    What did they say?

**Frank**    What did they say?

**Katie**    Yeah.

**Frank**    What did they say?

**Katie**    What did they say?

**Frank**    What did they say?

**Katie** *doesn't answer.*

What did they say?

**Katie** *doesn't answer.*

**Frank**    They didn't say anything.

**Katie**    Didn't they?

**Frank**    No. They hardly spoke to me.

**Katie**    Crikey.

**Frank**    They ignored me. They acted like I wasn't there. It was hard to ignore me as I was doing cartwheels across the room. They didn't like that. My cartwheels. Not at all. I milked it Kate. I shoved it right in their faces. Spotty herberts. I told them I said look kids, I said listen kids it's nothing personal, it's just business, Frank is taking care of business, that's all. That's all this is. Business. It's business. Business Kate. They didn't understand. They looked at me like I was talking Chinese. I said look kids, I don't know Chinese, alright, I wasn't too bright at school, languages wasn't my best subject, but whatever the Chinese is for business, translate that back into English and there you are, that's my point. Right there. In Chinese. 'Business'.

**Katie** *and* **Deanne** *look nonplussed.*

**Deanne**    Poor kids.

**Frank**    Fuck them.

*The entry phone goes.*

**Deanne**   Oh hello.

**Frank** *gets up and answers it.*

**Frank**   Hello?

**Frank** *buzzes downstairs open.*

**Deanne**   Is that her?

**Frank** *nods and sits back down on the sofa. They all stare at* **Rosanna** *as she walks on through the front door with an ice tray.*

Goodie I can get a drink.

**Deanne** *holds on to* **Frank** *as she gets up.*

**Frank**   Don't fall now.

**Deanne**   I won't.

**Deanne** *takes the ice tray off* **Rosanna**.

About time.

**Rosanna**   Innit.

**Deanne** *takes her glass and starts making herself a rum and coke with ice.*

You see Frank. That's how you get ice. You get the ice and you go and get it. No big secret.

**Deanne**   Gordon Ramsay would be proud of ya.

**Rosanna**   He would.

**Deanne**   He'd be more than a bit impressed.

**Rosanna**   *He's* age appropriate.

**Deanne**   What do you mean?

**Rosanna**   And he's got kids.

**Deanne** *looks nonplussed.*

He's ticking all the boxes.

**Deanne**   Bingo.

**Rosanna** *and* **Deanne** *crack up.*

**Rosanna**   I'd never have to cook another meal.

**Deanne**   Just as well.

**Rosanna** *and* **Deanne** *crack up.*

**Rosanna**   Imagine Dee.

**Deanne**   What?

**Rosanna**   I went out with Gordon Ramsay and you with Simon Cowell.

**Deanne**   Ooh don't.

**Rosanna**   And Kate went out with Frank.

**Rosanna** *and* **Deanne** *crack up while* **Katie** *laughs and* **Frank** *gives a look.*

**Deanne**   Ohh he's not that bad.

**Rosanna** *looks taken aback.*

**Rosanna**   Excuse me?

**Deanne**   Well.

**Rosanna**   What's 'not that bad' about him?

**Deanne** *looks at* **Frank** *and tries to think of something positive to say about him.*

**Deanne**   Well . . .

**Rosanna**   What?

**Deanne**   He's got . . .

**Rosanna**   Yeah?

**Deanne**   He's got . . .

**Rosanna**   What?

**Deanne**   You know . . .

**Rosanna**   No.

**Deanne** *nods like it's on the tip of her tongue.*

**Deanne**   Okay you win.

**Rosanna** *and* **Deanne** *crack up while* **Katie** *laughs and* **Frank** *gives a look.*

Go on then.

**Rosanna**   What?

**Rosanna** *suddenly realises what* **Deanne**'*s enquiring about.*

Oh yeah.

**Deanne**   Well?

**Rosanna**   I spoke to Dan.

**Deanne**   And?

**Rosanna**   He listened.

**Deanne**   And?

**Rosanna**   Spark's gone and he's upstairs doing his homework.

**Katie**   He isn't?

**Deanne**   It's Saturday night.

**Rosanna**   I don't care what night it is. I asked him if he wants to be like Frank. That soon focused his mind let me tell ya. You've never seen anyone bolt up them stairs so quick. Thanks Frank. By the way how's your pride?

**Frank**   My pride? It's fine.

**Rosanna**   I hear you took a hammering.

**Frank**   You what?

**Katie**   I thought you beat them?

**Rosanna**   Is that what he said?

**Frank**   I didn't say 'beat' them.

**Katie**   Murdered them you said.

**Frank**   It was close.

**Rosanna**   Close? They're still wetting their *pants* over it.

**Deanne**   Is it?

**Frank**   They talk shit.

**Katie**   Honestly you're such a child.

**Frank**   You're going to take their word over mine?

**Katie**   Yes.

**Frank**   They caught me on an off day. I had my mind on other things.

**Rosanna**   What, like getting the ice?

**Rosanna** *and* **Deanne** *crack up.* **Deanne** *gulps down her drink.*

**Deanne**   I tell you what I was thirsty.

**Rosanna**   No wonder. Have another one.

**Deanne**   I think I will. This time I'll put rum in it. That was just a thirst quencher.

**Rosanna**   Don't forget me.

**Deanne**   Oh sorry Dee.

**Rosanna**   You're Dee I'm Rose.

**Deanne**   Sorry Rose.

**Rosanna**   Here sit down.

**Deanne**   I think I will.

**Deanne** *leaves her glass in the kitchen and sits back down on the sofa.*

Is it stuffy in here or is it me?

**Rosanna**   I think it's you.

**Deanne**   Oh.

**Deanne** *looks a bit disorientated.*

It must be me.

**Rosanna** *makes* **Deanne** *a refill and gives it to her.*

Thanks.

**Rosanna** *takes her drink, adds ice, and has a sip.*

**Rosanna**    Bit flat.

**Deanne**    Is it?

**Rosanna**    Hmm.

**Deanne**    Mine's fine.

**Deanne** *gulps down her drink.*

'Nice with ice'.

**Deanne** *wipes her brow.*

I tell you what, a cold drink on a day like today. Fucking hell it's hot in here. Haven't you got air conditioning?

**Deanne** *holds out her glass for* **Rosanna**.

Top her up.

**Rosanna**    Blimey.

**Katie**    Don't let the grass grow.

**Deanne**    I'm thirsty. It was that Indian.

**Rosanna**    Hot?

**Deanne**    Not half. It's made me sweat like a pig look at me. I'm going to have to strip off in a minute.

**Deanne** *waits for a response.*

Frank.

**Frank**    What?

**Deanne**    Did you hear that? Me. No clothes. Think about it.

**Deanne** *cracks up.*

**Rosanna**   You've put the fear of god into him.

**Rosanna** *and* **Deanne** *crack up.*

**Deanne**   Ohh don't be so sensitive.

**Deanne** *strokes* **Frank**.

He's quite a sensitive little soul your Frank. He's quite a
delicate little butterfly.

**Deanne** *strokes* **Frank**.

Here do you want yours?

**Frank**   *Oi* . . .

**Frank** *whisks his plate from* **Deanne**'s *grasp.*

**Deanne**   Alright. No need to get uppity. Keep your hair on.
It's only food. It's only a bleeding curry. It's not like I even
like curry. I can't stand curry. Fucking curry. Curry's shit.

**Deanne** *looks miffed as* **Frank** *gets up with the plate.*

Here where you going with that curry?

**Frank** *starts preparing to reheat his food in the oven.*

Hel*lo*?

**Deanne** *holds out her glass for* **Rosanna** *who takes it and starts
making her a refill.*

You got a text.

**Rosanna**   *I* did?

**Deanne** *nods.*

Who from?

**Deanne**   Don't know.

**Rosanna**   Don't tell me you don't have a peek at my texts.

**Deanne**   Why should I? What could possibly happen in
your life that interests me?

**Rosanna**   You'll be surprised.

**Deanne**   Oh yeah?

**Rosanna**   Let's just see who it's from shall we?

**Deanne**   Are you expecting one?

**Rosanna**   Might be.

**Deanne**   Who from?

**Rosanna**   That would be telling.

**Rosanna** *gives* **Deanne** *her drink and sits down on the sofa with her drink.*

Are you ready for this?

**Deanne** *sidles up next to* **Rosanna**.

**Deanne**   What is it?

**Rosanna** *opens her text.*

**Rosanna**   Oh.

**Deanne**   What's up?

**Rosanna**   Miranda.

**Katie**   Who's that?

**Rosanna**   Olly's wife.

**Deanne**   Oh yeah?

**Rosanna**   What's she contacting me for? She never contacts me.

**Rosanna** *reads the text.*

**Frank**   Who's Olly?

**Katie**   The binman remember? I told you about him. Lost both his feet in an accident.

**Deanne**   Four kids.

**Katie**   He went in the back of the truck and it sliced them off.

**Frank**, **Katie** *and* **Deanne** *all grimace.*

**Deanne**   Well?

**Rosanna**   I can't make head or tail of this.

**Deanne**   What you doing?

**Rosanna** *presses call and puts the phone to her ear.*

**Rosanna**   Miranda? Rose. How you doing . . . ? You just sent me a text . . . ?

**Rosanna** *falls silent.*

*Was* my husband. You should worry about *your* husband. *He's* the one playing away from home. Can't think why.

**Rosanna** *scoffs and hangs up.*

Silly bitch.

**Deanne**   What's happened?

**Rosanna**   Jimmy.

**Deanne**   What's he done?

**Rosanna**   You're not going to believe this.

**Deanne**   What?

**Rosanna**   Him and Olly have been shagging a twenty year old.

**Deanne**   What?

**Rosanna**   *Together.*

**Deanne**   Together?

**Rosanna**   He's been filming them.

**Deanne**   What?

**Rosanna** *nods.*

Jimmy?

**Frank**   Cocaine.

**Rosanna**   It's all come out.

**Deanne**   How has it?

**Rosanna**   What if the boys find out?

**Katie**   They won't.

**Rosanna**   They might do. The dirty perverted . . .

**Deanne**   It's consensual.

**Rosanna**   He's an invalid. He hasn't got any feet. It's *sick*.

**Katie**   You said it.

**Rosanna**   How could he do this?

**Frank**   Cocaine.

**Katie**   This is going to affect Jimmy badly.

**Rosanna**   You what?

**Katie**   He's a proud man.

**Rosanna**   Proud? What about me?

**Frank**   It's got nothing to do with you. You have to let it go. Jimmy's on a downward spiral and he won't stop til he gets to the bottom.

**Deanne**   Oh Rose.

**Rosanna**   That fucking bitch. Taking it out on me. Just cos her husband's playing away from home. What's she telling *me* for Jimmy's not mine. She's a bitch.

**Katie**   Don't worry about her.

**Deanne**   Don't worry about any of them.

**Frank**   They're not worth it.

**Deanne**   Here have another drink.

**Rosanna**   I don't want a drink.

**Deanne**   Have a drinky.

**Rosanna**   I don't want one.

**Deanne**    Go on Rose have one.

**Rosanna**    I don't fucking want one.

**Deanne**    Alright.

**Rosanna**    Will you lay *off* me?

**Deanne**    I'm only offering you a drink. For fuck sake. You don't want a drink just say so. Why the big to-do?

**Rosanna**    Oh my fucking god.

**Rosanna** *gets up and starts pacing around.*

**Katie**    Shoes.

**Rosanna**    Oh fuck off.

**Rosanna** *takes off her shoes and tosses them on the floor.*

**Deanne**    Get us a refill.

**Rosanna**    Get it yourself.

**Deanne**    Charming.

**Deanne** *gets up and starts making herself a refill, finishing the bottle of rum.*

**Rosanna**    What am I going to do?

**Katie**    What can you do?

**Frank**    Do nothing.

**Rosanna**    Nothing? This is all going to come out.

**Frank**    So what?

**Katie**    It has nothing to do with you.

**Rosanna**    People will know.

**Katie**    Let them.

**Rosanna**    Let them?

**Katie**    That's right.

**Rosanna**    What, you mean the way you let everyone . . .

**Rosanna** *hesitates*.

Know about . . .

**Rosanna** *stops*.

**Katie**    That's different.

**Rosanna**    Why?

**Katie**    That was my business. Zane was my husband.

**Frank**    What's this got to do with Zane?

**Rosanna**    You don't know?

**Frank**    No.

**Rosanna**    Oh.

**Frank** *looks nonplussed*.

**Frank**    Well?

**Katie**    It doesn't matter.

**Frank**    No go on.

**Rosanna**    Leave it.

**Frank**    You brought it up.

**Katie**    Zane cheated on me. Okay. I've said it.

**Frank**    What?

**Frank** *looks nonplussed*.

When?

**Katie**    It doesn't matter.

**Frank**    With who?

**Katie**    It doesn't matter.

**Deanne**    Oh go on Kate tell us.

**Frank**    That was ages ago.

**Katie**    I know.

**Frank**  I'm sorry.

**Katie**  It's okay.

**Frank**  He was in the madness Kate. He *is* in the madness. He doesn't know what he's doing.

**Katie**  I know.

**Frank**  It's no reflection on you.

**Katie**  I know.

**Frank**  It's what addicts do. Addicts are never content with their lot. They'll always seek a way out in some way. It just so happens in Zane's case it was that way. He didn't mean no harm by it.

**Katie**  I know.

**Rosanna**  Don't start making excuses for him. A cheat's a cheat.

**Frank**  I'm not making excuses.

**Rosanna**  He's a filthy rotten cheat.

**Frank**  I'm not saying he's not.

**Katie**  Can we leave Zane out of this?

**Katie** *begins to cry.*

Can we please leave Zane out of this. For once.

*The others look nonplussed.*

**Rosanna**  Frankie.

**Frank**  What?

**Rosanna**  Tissues.

**Frank**  Where are they?

**Rosanna** *looks at* **Frank** *as if to say 'get your sorry arse over there'.*

I'm sorry Kate.

**Frank** *tries to comfort* **Katie**.

**Katie**   It's okay.

**Katie** *brushes* **Frank** *away*.

**Rosanna**   See what you've done?

*Frank looks nonplussed.*

**Frank**   Me?

**Rosanna**   We were fine before you walked in. We were having a good night. We were having the time of our lives.

**Deanne**   This is one of the best episodes in ages.

*Frank looks nonplussed.*

**Frank**   Don't blame me for Zane Rose.

**Rosanna** *smirks*.

Don't blame me for Jim.

**Rosanna**   You're all the same. You addicts. You only think of one thing. Yourselves. It's nothing personal Frank I like you you're Italian it's nothing personal. Kate don't want to be with you. She has no choice. She's drawn to the gutter through forces beyond her control. She's mad. And mad people need help. She'd go to meetings but you won't let her.

**Frank** *stares at* **Rosanna**.

**Katie**   It's okay Frank.

**Frank**   I'm fine.

**Katie**   I'm fine.

**Frank**   I'm sorry I was late.

**Katie**   I wasn't worried about *that*. I know you're not seeing someone else. I was worried about . . .

**Katie** *stops*.

**Frank**   I was fine. I was next door.

**Katie**   I know.

**Frank**   I was playing video games. They kept beating me. My pride kicked in.

**Frank** *and* **Katie** *laugh.*

Imagine being beaten by John Travolta. It's not good. They even offered me a points start. Can you believe that? Two spotty virgins offering *me* a points start? I felt like saying 'Look kids, I know you think you're John Travolta, okay, I know you think you're in the fucking movies, but first of all John Travolta doesn't have spots, okay, nothing personal, secondly he's been to bed with a woman, alright, allegedly, and thirdly you're just a pair of cunts.'

*The others look at* **Frank** *nonplussed.*

I didn't.

**Rosanna**   Good.

**Katie**   Get your food.

**Frank**   Fine.

**Frank** *walks back to the kitchen.* **Rosanna** *starts scrolling on her phone.*

**Katie**   What you doing?

**Rosanna**   Calling Jimmy.

**Katie**   Don't call Jimmy.

**Rosanna**   Why not?

**Katie**   Do you want a fight?

**Rosanna** *stops scrolling.*

**Rosanna**   You're right.

**Deanne**   Can you imagine?

**Rosanna**   Who is this girl?

**Deanne**   God knows.

**Rosanna**    I don't want to know.

**Katie**    That's the spirit.

**Rosanna**    Silly slag.

**Katie**    She's young she's impressionable.

**Rosanna**    She's a whore.

**Katie**    They've exploited her.

**Rosanna**    It's consensual.

**Deanne**    It's shameful.

**Rosanna**    It's shameful.

**Rosanna** *nods.*

She's young enough to be their daughter.

**Rosanna** *scowls.*

What a sick depraved lunatic.

**Frank**    Addict.

**Rosanna**    Sick depraved lunatic.

**Frank**    Same thing.

**Frank** *sits down on the sofa with a glass of apple juice with ice, his plate of reheated food and his fork, and starts eating.*

**Rosanna**    Do you remember what he was like Katie? Do you remember when I met him?

**Deanne** *nods.*

What's happened to that man?

**Deanne**    I don't know.

**Rosanna**    Disappeared. He was a go-getter. He was always doing things remember? He was ambitious. The only thing he goes and gets these days is coke. Everything is all about coke. That's his whole reason for living. He used to be interested in things. You could talk to him about anything.

He knew it all. Today all he's interested in is coke. How he can get it where he can get it how he can get the money. He doesn't care who he steps on. He has no scruples at all. He's a man possessed. If you were to tie him up, put him in a bag, padlock him, throw away the key, put the bag in the middle of the sea, you watch, he'd still get coke. I promise you. The drive of the man. And they say addicts lack willpower. What a load of tosh. If he put half as much effort into something useful as he does in getting coke, there'd be no stopping him. Literally no stopping him. He'd be running the country by now he's that single-minded. He was so good with the kids remember? Kind, loving, tender. Look at him now. It's as if they don't exist. He says he'll see them he forgets. He literally forgets. Forgets about his own kids. My Jimmy. He was beautiful. I'm not being funny but he was a looker. Have you seen him lately?

**Katie**   No.

**Deanne**   You don't want to.

**Katie**   Lost it?

**Deanne**   Not half.

**Rosanna**   He's fat he's bloated he's unwashed.

**Deanne**   His eyes are fucked.

**Rosanna**   He was always well turned out remember?

**Katie**   I do.

**Rosanna**   He was always polite. Always happy. Not anymore.

**Katie**   He had his moments.

**Rosanna**   Not like now. He was exciting. He was fun to be with. He was a good man. Had his moments but deep down he was good. Do you think I would have married a bad man I don't want a bad man that's not what floats my boat. I'm sorry. *You* can do all that not me.

**Deanne**'s *ringtone goes.*

**Deanne**    Oh hello.

**Rosanna**    That'll be her.

**Deanne**    Who?

**Rosanna**    Miranda. She'll be calling round telling everyone.

**Deanne**    Silly tart.

**Rosanna**    Fuck her.

**Deanne**    Fuck her.

**Rosanna**    You're right.

**Deanne**    Ignore her.

**Rosanna**    Ignore the call.

**Deanne**    I will.

**Rosanna**    No no you answer it.

**Deanne**    Why should I?

**Rosanna**    Let me speak to her.

**Deanne**    You speak to her.

**Rosanna**    No you speak to her.

**Deanne**    No you speak.

**Rosanna**    Tell her she's a whore.

**Deanne**    You tell her.

**Rosanna**    Pretend you don't know pretend I haven't spoken to you.

**Deanne**    I'll pretend I don't know you.

**Rosanna**    Pretend you don't know me. Don't pretend you don't know me she knows you know me.

**Deanne**    I'll pretend I don't know *her*.

**Rosanna**    Delete her from your phone.

**Deanne**   I *will* delete her from my phone. She's not even *on* my phone.

**Rosanna**   Is it her?

**Deanne**   Who knows?

**Rosanna**   Answer it.

**Deanne**   What should I say?

**Rosanna**   Tell her she's a *cunt*.

**Rosanna** *snatches the phone off* **Deanne** *and answers it.*

Hello . . . ? Yes you're a *cunt*. Did you hear that? Everyone in here thinks you're a *cunt*. Everyone in here thinks you're going to get your head kicked in. And *I'm* going to kick your head the hardest. I'm going to fucking smash it into *smithereens*.

**Rosanna** *looks nonplussed.*

Oh hello Officer.

**Deanne**   Officer?

**Rosanna** *holds out the phone for* **Deanne**.

**Rosanna**   Here it's for you.

**Deanne** *sits down on the sofa with her drink and takes the call.*

**Deanne**   Hello . . . ? Yes Officer that's my name . . . Yes he is my son.

**Katie**   Oh no.

**Deanne**   I see.

**Rosanna**   What's happened?

**Deanne**   I see.

**Rosanna**   You see what?

**Deanne** *holds back the emotion.*

**Deanne**   I'm sorry I can't.

**Katie**    Sorry you can't what?

**Rosanna**    What the fuck's happened?

**Deanne**    Thank you for telling me.

**Rosanna**    For telling you what?

**Katie**    Will you leave it.

**Deanne**    Thank you Officer . . . Yes . . . Goodbye.

**Deanne** *hangs up and composes herself while the others brace themselves.*

Victor.

**Rosanna**    What's happened to him?

**Deanne**    Arrested.

**Katie**    Phew.

**Rosanna**    Is that all?

**Deanne**    He was caught stealing a motorbike.

**Katie**    I didn't know he rode?

**Deanne**    He doesn't. Not as far as I know. Mind you I don't know him anymore do I? He could be a speedway champion for all I know.

**Katie**    Oh Dee.

**Deanne**    He's only just got out.

**Katie**    I know.

**Deanne**    I haven't even seen him. This time they're going to throw away the key.

**Katie**    They won't.

**Deanne**    They will. He's going to be in a long time what with his record. They're not going to be lenient. He's got a kid he's got a family he's got a mother. Me.

**Deanne** *breaks down.*

**Katie**  Come here.

**Katie** *gets up, sits down on the sofa beside* **Deanne** *and comforts her.*

**Rosanna**  Come here Dee.

**Rosanna** *sits down the other side of* **Deanne** *and comforts her, squashing* **Frank** *who's forced to get up, sitting down on the armchair instead with his fork, plate and glass.*

**Deanne**  They asked if I wanted to visit him. I wouldn't even know what he looks like. He wouldn't even want me to be there. His own mother. How sad. I'm an abject failure.

**Katie**  You're not.

**Deanne**  I am. Everything I've ever done has gone wrong. You tell me one good thing I've done.

**Katie**  You have four kids.

**Deanne**  All by different fathers. Anyone can have four kids by different fathers. All you have to do is sleep around a lot. I'm a fat slag.

**Katie**  How *dare* you speak about yourself like that.

**Deanne**  It's true.

**Katie**  It is not. You're an inspiration to me.

**Deanne**  *I* am?

**Katie**  You're one of the most remarkable people I've ever met. Rosie tell her.

**Rosanna**  It's true Dee.

**Deanne**  You're just humouring me.

**Katie**  I am not. I look up to you.

**Deanne**  *You* do?

**Katie**  You were brought up in care. You were abused. You were a mother by the age of thirteen. You were knocked about by your fella. You brought up four kids by yourself.

Nobody helped you bring them up. *You* brought them up.
Of course you've made mistakes. We *all* do. You're not
responsible for their shortcomings you're responsible for the
fact they've got any redeeming features at all. That was *you*
Dee. What sort of a life would they have had without you?
You dragged yourself up by the heels and did something
with yourself. You showed them what was possible. You
taught yourself to read and write. To read and write Dee.
Nobody taught you for you. *You* taught you. You went to
college you got a degree. More than Rosanna ever got.

**Rosanna**   Oi hold up.

**Katie**   You got yourself a job helping other women.
Women who had suffered the same fate as you.

**Deanne**   I was good at that job.

**Katie**   You were.

**Deanne**   I worked hard for it.

**Katie**   You did.

**Deanne**   No-one gave me a helping hand.

**Katie**   That's right.

**Deanne**   And what happened? Huh? Ask yourself that?
What happened?

**Katie**   That was just bad luck.

**Deanne**   You could say that.

**Katie**   Someone just had it in for you that's all.

**Deanne**   Why me though?

**Katie**   I don't know.

**Deanne**   How could they make that allegation against me?
Sexual harassment. Against a woman. Me? I'm as straight as
the day is long.

**Katie**   These things happen.

**Deanne**   Why do they always happen to me? Why me? What did I do that was so god damn awful? What did I do to deserve all this shit? Answer that.

**Rosanna**   Those allegations were proved false. You were given back your job.

**Deanne**   *Fuck* their job. I don't *want* their job.

**Rosanna**   They had no alternative but to suspend you.

**Deanne**   Are you siding with them?

**Rosanna**   I'm not siding with them.

**Deanne**   Maybe they could have backed me up.

**Rosanna**   Maybe they didn't want to.

**Deanne**   That's the point.

**Rosanna**   That *is* the point. Maybe they had to take the allegation seriously.

**Deanne**   But they knew me.

**Rosanna**   What did they know about you?

**Deanne**   I'm a hard worker.

**Rosanna**   That don't make you perfect.

**Deanne**   So you believe them?

**Rosanna**   Of course I don't.

**Deanne**   We know what happened.

**Rosanna**   What happened?

**Deanne**   Someone was jealous.

**Rosanna**   Who?

**Deanne**   Someone in the office. I don't know. I was new I was good I was going straight to the top. They could see that. They felt threatened. They gave the allegations merit. When they knew it was a pack of lies. That's what happened. I could have been somebody. They knew that. They wanted to keep me in my place.

**Rosanna**   Looks like they succeeded.

**Deanne**   Fuck them.

**Katie**   You take things too personally. You think everyone's out to get you.

**Deanne**   How would *you* take it?

**Rosanna**   I'd go back. I'd feel vindicated.

**Deanne**   I wouldn't go back there if you paid me.

**Katie**   That's just pride.

**Deanne**   That's self-respect. I respect myself too much to go back. Here get me a drink.

**Katie**   You don't respect yourself too much to drink.

**Deanne**   What? Oh shut up will you.

**Katie**   It's true.

**Deanne**   Stop with the lectures. I've had enough of them.

**Frank**   We're all out.

**Deanne**   What?

**Frank**   The rum's gone.

**Deanne**   It has not?

**Frank**   Fraid so.

**Deanne**   That can't be right.

**Frank**   It is.

**Deanne**   Well get some more.

**Frank**   We don't have more.

**Deanne**   Well get some.

**Frank**   *You* get some.

**Deanne**    Fuck me am I the only one who's got any initiative?

**Deanne** *gets up.*

Of *course* you've got a drink. Look in the cupboards.

**Deanne** *starts pulling open the cupboards.*

**Frank**    There's none there.

**Deanne**    You'll have some of those small liqueurs. For cooking.

**Frank**    We don't have any.

**Deanne**    You don't have any small liqueurs?

**Frank**    No.

**Deanne**    You call this a kitchen?

**Deanne** *looks nonplussed.*

Rose what have you got?

**Rosanna**    Nothing.

**Deanne**    You've got no alcohol in your house? What kind of establishment is it?

**Rosanna**    It's a house.

**Deanne** *looks nonplussed.*

**Deanne**    Go down the shop.

**Rosanna**    Perhaps you need a break.

**Deanne**    What?

**Rosanna**    Perhaps Katie's right.

**Deanne**    I've just been told my son's going down.

**Rosanna**    Precisely.

**Katie**    Maybe it's time to sober up.

**Deanne**    I can't believe I'm hearing this. You lot are torturing me.

**Katie**   We are not.

**Deanne**   Here Frank give me some money.

**Frank**   What for?

**Deanne**   Just give me.

**Frank**   No.

**Deanne**   I'll pay you back.

**Frank**   That's not the point.

**Deanne**   But I need a drink.

**Katie**   I thought you had booze at your place?

**Deanne**   Are you kidding? I haven't got anything. I wish I had something I like drinking at home. I far prefer it. For one thing it's cheaper and for another you don't have to share. I don't have to make idle talk when there's serious drinking to be done. I can't keep anything for more than two minutes. No sooner is it there than it's gone. And the sad thing is, the next day, I can't remember drinking it. I know I drank it cos I can see the bottles. I can feel my head. I can smell the piss in my bed.

**Rosanna**   Is that really necessary?

**Deanne**   But I can't remember drinking it. I can't remember putting the thing to my lips. I think I've got a problem.

**Rosanna**   You could say that.

**Deanne**   I can't stop drinking.

**Frank**   It's alright.

**Deanne**   It's not alright. I need to stop but I can't. I want to stop. So badly. I've been wanting to stop for umpteen years. Every morning I wake up I tell myself I'm going to stop. I mean it. I mean it with every ounce of my body. I tell myself you're not going to have one today. Even if it kills you you're not going to have one. Then the thought enters. Out of nowhere. Just pops in. I try to make it go away but I can't. Sometimes I sit there trying not to think about it. I think about it. I wonder how people can sit there *without* thinking about it. I don't know how to. I don't know how to remove the obsession. Most of the time the thought enters I don't even think those things. I only think of one thing. A drink. A teeny weeny drink. I promise myself it'll only be one. But it's never one. It's always more. More and more and more and more. Until I'm conked out or until it's all out. Then I go to bed. My heart bleeding. My head hurting. My sordid little world. My sordid little shame. I can't look myself in the mirror the next day. I avoid contact with my eyes. Because the eyes know. I can kid myself all I want but the eyes know. The eyes have seen it all. Somebody help me.

**Frank**    I'll help you.

**Deanne**    Will you?

**Frank**    Of course I will. You've made a very important step. You've admitted you've got a problem. I'll take you to meetings.

**Deanne**    I can't go to meetings.

**Frank**    Why not?

**Deanne**    Looking like this?

**Frank**    You look fine.

**Deanne**    I don't want anyone to see me.

**Frank**    That's how everyone feels when they go in.

**Deanne**    Let me start the new regime first.

**Frank**    There is no new regime Dee. It's the same *old* regime time after time. Take a look at your life. Is it one big long old regime?

**Deanne** *nods*.

Does nothing change? Does everything just get worse?

**Deanne**    It does.

**Frank**    Well then.

**Deanne**    You're right.

**Frank**    It ain't going to get any better.

**Deanne**    I just want to drink normally. I want to know how to have one and not go on a binge.

**Frank**    You can't. Those days are over.

**Deanne**    I want to know how to have a little tipple at Christmas.

**Frank**    You can't.

**Deanne**    And weekends.

**Frank**    I'm sorry.

**Deanne**    I want to know how to not drink myself to oblivion.

**Frank**    By not drinking at all.

**Deanne**    How do I do that?

**Frank**    I'll take you to meetings.

**Katie**    Will you go Dee?

**Frank**    I'll take you to one now if you want.

**Deanne**'s *face drops.*

**Deanne**    During The X Factor?

**Katie**    It's about to finish.

**Deanne**    What sort of people go to meetings during The X Factor?

**Frank**    Alcoholics.

**Deanne** *looks crestfallen.*

**Deanne**    Alcoholics?

**Frank**    That's right.

**Deanne**    Alcoholics?

**Frank**   That's right.

**Deanne**   No no. I'm not doing that. I'm not hanging out with those people. I've got my reputation.

**Rosanna**   You certainly have.

**Deanne**   Nothing against them. I'm sure they're very nice people. I'm sure they're the life and soul of the party. I'm sure they're a bundle of laughs. That's not me. I'm fine I'm a mother I've got a house. I've got a job. I've got my fucking head.

**Frank**   It's up to you. I can't force you. Do what you want Dee. I'm always here if you need me.

**Deanne**   Let me just have a drink.

**Frank**   I ain't got one.

**Deanne**   Rosie let me have your drink.

**Rosanna**   You've had enough.

**Deanne**   One more. One more and that's it. I'll give up. I promise I'll have no more after that.

**Rosanna**   Here have it.

**Deanne** *takes* **Rosanna**'s *drink off her and gulps it down.*

**Deanne**   One more to celebrate.

**Rosanna** *shakes her head.*

That's it?

**Rosanna**   That's it.

**Deanne**   No more?

**Rosanna**   No more.

**Deanne**   You crafty bugger.

**Frank**   What?

**Deanne**   Look at you.

**Frank**    What about me?

**Deanne**    Pretending you'll help me.

**Frank**    I *will* help you.

**Deanne**    You sneaky rascal.

**Deanne** *snatches* **Frank**'s *drink off the coffee table.*

Nothing more to drink? You got to watch this one.

**Deanne** *laughs as if to say 'nothing gets past me', gulps down the rest of the drink, and spits it out.*

What the fuck's that?

**Frank**    Apple juice.

**Deanne**    Apple juice? With no rum in it? How can you drink apple juice without rum? Rum and apple it's a classic.

**Katie** *gets up, puts* **Rosanna**'s *and* **Frank**'s *empty glasses by the sink, gets the cloth, and starts cleaning up the apple juice.* **Deanne** *practically retches.*

I bet you I've got apple juice poisoning.

**Katie** *puts the cloth by the sink, dries her hands with the tea towel, and sits back down on the sofa.*

I suppose I'll just sit down then.

**Katie**    You do that.

**Deanne**    Don't mind me.

**Katie**    I won't.

**Deanne**    I've only just been given some terrible news.

**Katie**    That's as may be.

**Deanne**    Does no-one care? My son's a diabetic my other son's a serial offender. Is it any wonder I drink?

**Katie**    They're not the reason you drink. *You* are.

**Deanne**  Oh that's right blame me. If there's a problem blame Deanne she'll cop the flak she always does. Put it on her. I tell you what why don't you all kill me now. I feel like I'm everyone's punch bag.

**Katie**'s *ringtone goes*.

**Katie**  That'll be Chrissie.

**Deanne**  You better take it Kate.

**Katie** *looks nonplussed*.

**Katie**  Of *course* I'm going to take it. It's not all about *you* you know.

**Deanne**  That's right.

**Deanne** *sits down on the sofa*.

Kick a girl when she's down.

**Katie** *answers the call*.

**Katie**  Hello . . . ? Hello angel . . . Did you watch it . . . ? Did you . . . ? Do you think she's going to win . . . ? I didn't really watch it that closely . . . The usuals. You know. Frank, Rose, Dee . . . Are you okay . . . ? How's daddy . . . ? Is he . . . ? Is she . . . ? Are they? Oh that's not good . . . Do you want to come home . . . ? You know it's okay if you do . . . ? Are you sure . . . ? I promise . . . Of course I do . . . Don't worry . . . Okay. I love you . . . I love you . . . Goodnight.

**Katie** *hangs up*.

**Rosanna**  What's happened?

**Katie**  Who said anything's happened?

**Rosanna**  What's up?

**Katie**  Nothing.

**Rosanna**  Katie.

**Katie**  They've been rowing.

**Frank**   Zane and Minny?

**Rosanna**   Over what?

**Katie**   I don't know.

**Rosanna**   Have they been shouting?

**Katie**   I don't know. I couldn't hear anything going on. Mind you they'd shut up when she phoned me.

**Frank**   Is she okay?

**Katie**   She seems weird.

**Rosanna**   Go and get her.

**Katie**   I can't. She wants to be there. It's her dad's night.

**Frank**   Call her dad.

**Katie**   I can't.

**Rosanna**   Why not?

**Katie**   I promised her. I promised her I wouldn't call.

**Frank**   Call him Kate.

**Katie**   She doesn't want him to know she said anything.

**Frank**   You need to know for your own peace of mind.

**Katie**   Look, they had a row. She doesn't know Minny that well.

**Rosanna**   Does she like her?

**Katie**   She loves her. She thinks the sun shines out of her arse. It was okay for Zane to remarry but not for me.

**Rosanna**   That's normal.

**Katie**   She worries about him.

**Rosanna**   She wants him to be happy.

**Katie**   I know that. It's just a bit weird when they row. It's not a secure environment.

**Frank**    It's not like when *we* row she knows she's safe.

**Frank** *looks nonplussed.*

What?

**Katie**    Do you really think that?

**Frank**    Of course.

**Katie**    Don't be so deluded.

**Frank**    What?

**Katie**    She doesn't know anything.

**Frank**    Doesn't she?

**Katie**    No.

**Frank**    Oh.

**Rosanna**    Oh indeed.

**Katie**    Bear that in mind next time you kick off.

**Frank** *looks nonplussed.*

**Frank**    Me?

**Katie** *gives a look.*

Do you want to go round there?

**Katie**    No.

**Frank**    You're well within your rights.

**Katie**    She's fine.

**Rosanna**    Are you sure?

**Frank**    I'm not going to have you staying up half the night worrying.

**Katie**    I won't.

**Frank**    Suffering.

**Katie**    I don't do that.

**Frank**    You do. You either do something about it or you let it go.

**Katie**    I've let it go.

**Frank**    Okay.

*They all gaze at the telly.*

**Katie**    Let me just call him.

**Katie** *starts making a call.*

No.

**Katie** *stops the call.*

I'm fine. She's fine. I'm worrying unduly.

**Frank**    Are you sure?

**Katie**    I'm sure.

**Frank**    You promise me?

**Katie**    Yes.

*They all gaze at the telly.*

**Frank**    For fuck sake.

**Rosanna**    What's up?

**Frank**    This always happens.

**Rosanna**    What does?

**Frank**    Now I can't relax because *you* can't relax.

**Katie**    I am relaxed.

**Frank**    You're not. You're worried about her. Now I have to worry about you worrying about her.

**Katie**    Don't start.

**Frank**    I'm not starting.

**Katie**    You are.

**Frank**    It's not my fault you don't trust her to be with her dad. Why have I got to suffer?

**Katie**    You're turning this all around.

**Frank**    Why does that have to impinge upon my fun? What have I done? I haven't done anything. I didn't marry him I didn't have a kid with him.

**Katie**    You married me and I came with Chrissie and Zane's Chrissie's father. You knew all that.

**Frank**    I didn't know he was going to spoil my Saturday night. It didn't say *that* on the tin.

**Katie**    This is absurd.

**Frank**    Is it?

**Rosanna**    *Yes* it is.

**Katie**    You're acting like a spoilt brat.

**Frank**    Why can't we have one night where Zane doesn't interfere? Where Zane actually meets his responsibilities so we can actually chill out on an evening without having to do our nut? Huh? Chrissie consumes more of your energy when she's at her dad's than when she's at home. Is that right? Do you think when she's here he spares her a single thought? Do you? He can't even remember her existence.

**Katie**    That's not true.

**Rosanna**    He has a point Katie.

**Frank**    He only has her two nights a week. That's when he's not touring. Or at a party. Or at an awards ceremony. Two nights and he can't even do that properly. And when she *does* stay there you still take her to school the next day. You. He can't be bothered to get up early enough. You still make her packed lunch. What is it he actually does?

**Katie**    He's her father.

**Frank**    And?

**Katie**   He loves her.

**Frank**   I thought love is a doing word? Isn't that what you always say?

**Katie**   He's unwell. Remember when you were unwell? Remember what you were like? I don't remember you rising bright and early every morning. Was love a doing word then?

**Frank**   That's different.

**Katie**   Why?

**Frank**   I didn't have a child.

**Katie**   No but *I* had a child and you could have helped out. I didn't have enough hours in the day. Meanwhile what were you doing? If anyone should understand Zane it should be you.

**Frank** *gets up and puts his finished plate of food and fork by the sink.*

Call Freddie he'll soon knock some sense into you.

**Rosanna**   Who's Freddie?

**Katie**   His sponsor.

**Rosanna**   Call Freddie.

**Frank**   I will.

**Rosanna**   You do that.

**Frank**   I will.

**Rosanna**   Tell him you're not well.

**Katie** *smirks.*

**Katie**   He already knows.

**Frank** *makes a call from his mobile.*

**Rosanna**   Maybe he shouldn't call Freddie.

**Katie**   What?

**Rosanna**   One phone call each and look.

**Katie**    He speaks to Freddie every day.

**Rosanna**    I bet you he's got cancer.

**Frank**    Freddie?

**Rosanna**    I bet you.

**Frank**    How you doing?

**Rosanna**    He's probably been run over by a bus.

**Frank**    I'm fine.

**Rosanna**    You watch.

**Katie**    I thought you were expecting some good news?

**Frank**    What?

**Katie**    That text.

**Frank**    Oh yeah.

**Katie**    What was all that about?

**Rosanna**    Promise you won't tell anyone?

**Katie**    What?

**Rosanna** *lowers her voice.*

**Rosanna**    I have an admirer.

**Deanne**'s *face drops.*

**Deanne**    What?

**Katie**    You never said.

**Deanne**    Who is he?

**Katie**    That's a turn-up for the books.

**Rosanna**    I met him on the internet.

**Katie**    You never did?

**Rosanna**    Twenty-seven.

**Deanne**    How old?

**Katie**    You cradle snatcher.

**Katie** *laughs while* **Rosanna** *and* **Deanne** *crack up.*

**Deanne**    How many times have you met?

**Rosanna**    We haven't.

**Deanne**    What?

**Rosanna**    We've spoken on the phone.

**Deanne**    And?

**Rosanna**    'Not bad'.

**Deanne**    Oh my God.

**Katie** *laughs while* **Rosanna** *and* **Deanne** *crack up.*

**Rosanna**    Pretty fucking impressive actually.

**Deanne**    Oh my God.

**Katie** *laughs while* **Rosanna** *and* **Deanne** *crack up.*

**Frank**    Oi can you guys keep it down.

**Katie**    Is he single?

**Rosanna**    Of course he is.

**Katie**    How do you know?

**Rosanna**    He told me.

**Katie**    So?

**Rosanna**    I've seen his profile. He wouldn't lie to me.

**Katie**    Wouldn't he?

**Rosanna**    Not if he knows what's good for him.

**Katie**    People lie on the net all the time.

**Rosanna**    It was on the phone Kate. I'm a very good judge of character.

**Katie**    You don't know him from Adam.

**Rosanna**    Not for long.

**Deanne**    What do you mean?

**Rosanna**    We've arranged a date.

**Deanne**    You haven't?

**Rosanna** *nods.*

When?

**Rosanna**    I don't know. He said he'd text me. I'm still waiting. I think he's having second thoughts. Mind you *I'd* have second thoughts if I were him. I'm *ravenous.*

**Rosanna** *and* **Deanne** *crack up.*

**Katie**    You be careful Rose.

**Rosanna**    Oh for fuck sake Kate you're such a killjoy. Heaven forbid I should have a bit of fun.

**Deanne**    Let the girl be.

**Rosanna**    Thank you Dee.

**Deanne**    She's not hurting anyone.

**Katie**    Please yourself.

**Rosanna**    Just because you're in a humdrum marriage doesn't mean we *all* have to be miserable.

**Deanne**    That's right.

**Rosanna**    Who wants commitment? Indian takeaways in front of The X Factor?

**Katie**    What's wrong with that?

**Rosanna**    He's taking me out. When was the last time Frank took you out?

**Deanne**    Exactly.

**Rosanna**    Thank you.

**Rosanna** *nods.*

Silence speaks . . .

**Rosanna** *can't find the end of the saying.*

**Deanne** That's right.

**Frank**   Okay Freddie . . . Thanks . . . Bye.

**Frank** *hangs up.*

**Katie**   Frank?

**Frank** *doesn't answer.*

What's up?

**Frank**   Rich.

**Katie**   Who's Rich?

**Frank**   Rich who was round here Sunday.

**Katie**   Your friend from the rooms?

**Frank**   That's right.

**Katie**   What about him?

**Frank**   Died.

**Katie**   You what?

**Rosanna**   Died?

**Katie**   How?

**Frank**   Heart failure.

**Katie**   Oh no.

**Rosanna**   What happened?

**Frank**   He was at home. With his wife. The kids asleep.

**Katie**   Kids?

**Frank**   He has another on the way. She's eighteen weeks pregnant.

**Katie**   She isn't?

**Frank** He tells her he's going to have a pipe. Just one hit.

**Katie** I thought he was clean?

**Frank** He was. Two and a half years.

**Katie** Oh my god.

**Frank** He tells her it's just one hit he'll be back in the rooms tomorrow to pick up his white chip and she should go upstairs. She goes upstairs, goes to bed, hears a thud. He's collapsed. Collapsed from a single pipe.

**Katie** He was younger than you.

**Frank** I know.

**Rosanna** How could he do that to her? How could he do that to the kids? What is it with men? Selfish. The lot of them.

**Frank** He was a good man.

**Rosanna** *smirks.*

He was my friend.

**Katie** I'm sorry Frank.

**Deanne** Dead?

**Frank** Dead.

**Deanne** Dead?

**Frank** That's what happens.

**Deanne** Dropped dead with no warning?

**Frank** That's right.

**Deanne** Surely there was something wrong with him?

**Frank** He was fine.

**Deanne** Dodgy ticker?

**Frank** Picture of health.

**Deanne** That's why I don't do drugs. You see. Glass of wine that's it. Drop of brandy perhaps. I won't do drugs.

The government should do something about it. They want to lock him up.

**Frank**    He's dead.

**Deanne** *looks nonplussed.*

**Deanne**    He's dead?

**Frank**    That's right.

**Deanne**    That's terrible.

**Frank**    It is.

**Deanne**    I wish there was something I could do.

**Frank**    There is.

**Deanne**    What?

**Frank**    Recover.

**Deanne** *doesn't answer.*

You can recover Dee. Give their children back their mum. Where's their mum been all this time? Where's she been hiding?

**Deanne**    Don't say that Frank. Please don't say that. I'm in enough pain as it is.

**Deanne** *begins to cry.*

**Frank**    He was only round here Sunday. He seemed well.

**Katie**    Just goes to show.

**Frank**    I know.

**Katie**    It doesn't matter how clean you are. Or how much you know.

**Frank**    I know that.

**Katie**    Let that be a wake-up call.

**Frank** *doesn't answer.*

Frank. Let that be a wake-up call. Do you hear?

**Katie** *begins to cry.*

**Frank**    Poor Rich.

**Rosanna**    Poor wife and kids more like. How come you never talk about them? Have you any idea what it's like for them?

**Frank**    I do.

**Rosanna** *smirks.*

**Rosanna**    Oh yeah?

**Frank**    That's how I lost my dad.

**Rosanna**    Oh.

**Frank** *doesn't answer.*

I'm sorry.

**Frank**    So you know.

**Rosanna**    I'm sorry Frank. I had no idea.

**Frank**    That's the way it goes.

**Frank**'s *eyes well up.*

Poor dad.

**Frank** *begins to cry.*

**Rosanna**    Bloody hell this is a jolly place.

**Rosanna** *looks around at everyone crying.*

I only came round to watch The X Factor.

**Rosanna** *looks nonplussed.*

Fuck me.

**Rosanna** *considers what to do.*

Here Dee we better go.

**Deanne**    What?

**Rosanna** *wipes* **Deanne**'s *eyes.*

**Rosanna**    Time to shoo.

**Rosanna** *gets up, puts her shoes on, and collects her mobile.*

**Deanne**    Are we going past the offy?

**Rosanna**    We're going back to mine.

**Deanne**    If we go back to mine we go past the offy.

**Rosanna***'s face drops.*

**Rosanna**    After everything that's happened?

**Deanne**    What's happened?

**Rosanna***'s face drops.*

**Rosanna**    What's happened?

**Deanne**    Tonight of all nights tomorrow I'll stop. A lot has happened tonight Rose. A lot. I don't know if you've been paying attention.

**Deanne** *starts sobbing.*

**Rosanna**    We'll go back to yours.

**Deanne**    Goodie.

**Deanne** *immediately perks up and reaches for her shoes.*

**Rosanna**    We'll watch the results there.

**Deanne**    What results? We don't need to watch the results. We know who's going out.

**Rosanna**    Who?

**Deanne**    That black one.

**Rosanna**    She's good.

**Deanne**    I know she's good. That's the point. She's talented she's beautiful she's black. She doesn't have a chance. Not with Dannii around. She's everything that Dannii's *not*. Work it out.

**Rosanna**    Get your shoes.

**Deanne**   Plastic Australian minger. That Simon Cowell needs his head testing. They may as well call that show Shoot The Black Person. Get The Black Person Up Against A Wall And Shoot Them.

**Deanne** *puts on her shoes, collects her mobile, and gets up.*

Let's go.

**Rosanna**   We're out of here.

**Rosanna** *wipes* **Katie***'s eyes.*

**Katie**   Thanks for coming.

**Deanne**   Don't get up.

**Katie**   I'll see ya.

**Rosanna**   See you later Katie.

**Deanne**   Bye Frank.

**Frank**   Girls.

**Rosanna**   See you soon.

**Frank**   Night.

**Rosanna** *walks up to* **Frank** *and wipes his eyes.*

**Rosanna**   Here Frank? What about Italy? Put those jocks to the sword. Come on. Let's have a smile.

**Frank**   Just scraped through.

**Rosanna**   We always just scrape through. Then we go and win the darn thing. We're going to win those Euros. You watch.

**Frank**   That we will.

**Rosanna**   We're the best. We're the best cooks the best lovers the best looking . . .

**Frank**   Enough about me.

**Rosanna**   The others haven't got a chance.

**Frank**   We'll see.

**Rosanna**   Forza Italia.

**Rosanna** *gives* **Frank** *a peck on both cheeks.*

**Frank**   Night night.

**Deanne** *walks up to* **Frank** *and wipes his eyes even though they've already been wiped.*

**Deanne**   Listen Frank. About your mate.

**Frank**   What about him?

**Deanne**   I'm sorry.

**Frank**   It's okay.

**Deanne**   Terrible business.

**Frank**   It is.

**Deanne**   Forget my woes for a second.

**Frank**   I have.

**Deanne**   We all have our own troubles.

**Frank**   We do.

**Deanne**   Let's hear no more of it.

**Frank**   No more of what?

**Deanne**   Whatever.

**Frank**   I'm not with you.

**Deanne**   Here give us a kiss you ol scally.

**Frank**   What?

**Deanne** *grabs* **Frank**'s *face and gives him a kiss on either cheek.*

**Deanne**   Don't fight it Frank. You know you want to.

**Deanne** *grabs* **Frank**'s *face again and plants a kiss on his lips.*

Ooh he's such a good-looking fella. You want to watch him Kate. That face. Ooh let me give it a kiss.

**Deanne** *grabs* **Frank***'s face again and plants another kiss on his lips.*

Beautiful. He's beautiful. I want him now.

**Rosanna** *and* **Deanne** *crack up.*

I've got to have him Kate you don't mind?

**Katie**    Go ahead.

**Deanne** *starts trying to undo* **Frank***'s trousers.*

**Frank**    Oi hold up.

**Frank** *starts fending her off.*

**Deanne**    That face. Look at that face.

**Deanne** *grabs* **Frank***'s face again and squashes his cheeks.*

**Frank**    Ow.

**Deanne**    Oh shut up you ol tart.

**Frank**    *Ow.*

**Deanne** *lets go of* **Frank***'s face.*

Fucking *hell.*

**Deanne**    Shut it.

**Deanne** *gives* **Frank** *two or three playful but hard slaps.*

**Frank**    Get *off.*

**Rosanna** *and* **Deanne** *crack up.*

**Rosanna**    See ya.

**Deanne**    'Wouldn't want to *be* ya'.

**Rosanna** *grabs* **Deanne** *and starts dragging her away.*

Katie Katie Katie.

**Katie**    What?

**Deanne**    Same time next week.

**Katie** *looks nonplussed.*

'Be there or be square.'

**Katie** *gets up and closes the front door behind* **Rosanna** *and* **Deanne** *as they walk off hollering.* **Frank** *looks at her as if to say 'blooming heck'.*

**Katie**    That was eventful.

**Frank**    You could say that.

*They laugh.*

Are you alright?

**Katie**    I'm fine.

**Frank**    I'm sorry I turned on you.

**Katie**    That's alright.

**Frank**    I was bang out of order. I just got fed up. I twisted everything round in my mind.

**Katie**    As you're prone to do.

*They laugh.*

**Frank**    I think you should phone Zane.

**Katie**    What?

**Frank**    You need to speak to him. It's no good you worrying about Chrissie.

**Katie**    I promised her.

**Frank**    It doesn't matter. She's just a child. You're not betraying her. You're looking out for her. It's the right thing to do.

**Katie**    I'm sure she's alright.

**Frank**    Of course she is. But you need to make sure.

**Katie**    You won't resent me?

**Frank**    I promise.

**Katie**    Thanks.

**Katie** *gives* **Frank** *a hug.*

You know Frank. I'm worried about her.

**Frank**  No?

**Katie** *laughs.*

**Katie**  Her self-esteem.

**Frank**  What about it?

**Katie**  It's low.

**Frank**  How do you know?

**Katie**  She's insecure. She worries what the other girls think. All the time.

**Frank**  That's normal.

**Katie**  It's not. She does whatever she thinks she needs to to fit in. She hasn't got a sense of self.

**Frank**  I see.

**Katie**  I catch her lying.

**Frank**  Lying about what?

**Katie**  About things going on at school.

**Frank**  What things?

**Katie**  Things with the other girls. She's desperately needy. I don't know how to improve her confidence.

**Frank**  You need to tell her not to lie.

**Katie**  I know.

**Frank**  You need to explain why.

**Katie**  The other day. She fell out with Beth and Suzy.

**Frank**  Why?

**Katie**  They were whispering.

**Frank**  About what?

**Katie**   I don't know. Nothing. She thought they were whispering about her. They weren't. They're her friends.

**Frank**   What did she do?

**Katie**   She accused them of talking about her. They denied it. Told her they were whispering about god knows what. Some stupidness. She didn't believe them. She finds Jane and Cassy.

**Frank**   Tells them what?

**Katie**   They're not even her friends. She shouldn't be telling them anything. They're not nice to her. She so desperately wants to be in with them she tells them her friends have been talking about her. When they haven't. Those girls will only use it against her you know what they're like. Meanwhile her *real* friends will desert her. She has to be careful.

**Frank**   You need to tell her.

**Katie**   I have.

**Frank**   What happened?

**Katie**   There was a lot of resistance. In the end she broke down. Admitted it.

**Frank**   She can always go back to them and say sorry.

**Katie** *nods*.

**Katie**   I'll tell her that.

**Frank**   No harm done. They'll respect her. Fuck what the other girls think.

**Katie**   Try telling *her* that. She worries desperately about what they think.

**Frank**   She mustn't compromise herself just to please them. That will only make her lose herself more. Tell her she's fine as she is we love her as she is.

**Katie**   It's about her loving herself. Perhaps her father's impacted on her negatively.

**Frank**    Yeah and perhaps she gets it off you.

**Katie**    That's true.

*They laugh.*

Sorry about Rich.

**Frank** *shakes his head*.

Such a nice fella.

**Frank**    The best.

**Katie**    It's awful.

**Frank**    I can't believe it.

**Katie**    Poor thing.

**Frank**    But for the grace of God.

**Katie**    Don't say that.

**Katie** *hugs* **Frank** *tight.*

**Frank**    That was me Katie. I came that close. Remember it like it were yesterday.

**Katie**    Don't ever forget.

**Frank**    Difficult to forget when you hear things like that.

**Katie**    You have a built-in forgetter.

**Frank**    Oh yeah I forgot.

*They laugh.*

**Katie**    You know Frank. I been thinking.

**Frank**    Oh fuck.

**Katie**    Why don't you write.

**Frank**    What?

**Katie**    It's good for you. Why don't you do it.

**Frank**    What's brought this on?

**Katie**   It's what you want to do. Do it.

**Frank**   It's not that simple.

**Katie**   Why not?

**Frank**   It's not up to me.

**Katie**   Who's it up to?

**Frank**   God.

**Katie**   God wants you to write. What else does he want you to do?

**Frank**   I was thinking of starting my own business.

**Katie**   Doing what?

**Frank**   Delivering ice.

**Katie** *gives a look.*

I think I found my calling.

**Katie**   Shut up.

**Frank**   What would I write about?

**Katie**   Ask Him.

**Frank**   I don't know anything. I only know how to stick pins in my eyes.

**Katie**   Write about that.

**Frank**   Nah.

**Katie**   Why not?

**Frank**   Who wants to hear about that?

**Katie**   Plenty people. Plenty people need to. Maybe that's why God made you go through all those terrible things. So you could come out the other side and write about them.

**Frank**   You think?

**Katie**   It's possible. Maybe he wanted you to value what you had. Maybe all the best things in the world aren't worth anything unless you value them. When you had it all, were you grateful?

**Frank** *thinks about it.*

**Frank**   I had a sense of entitlement. Like the world owed me. I didn't want anything the world had to give. Whatever it was it was wrong. I was angry.

**Katie**   You nearly paid with your life.

**Frank** *nods.*

Some people have nothing. And they're still grateful. You had to learn the value of things. You do now.

**Frank**   It's hard.

**Katie** *nods.*

Coming to terms with it all.

**Katie**   Think of others.

**Frank**   Yeah.

**Katie**   Everyone has sadness. Everyone has pain. It doesn't mean you have to rip yourself to shreds.

**Frank**   I suppose.

**Katie**   Think of all the good things you have. Your life's not over. It's all ahead of you. A second chance. That's what recovery gives you.

**Frank** *nods.*

Think of Bubba.

**Frank**   I do.

**Katie**   You're blessed.

**Frank**   I know.

**Katie**   That boy needs you.

**Frank**   I know.

**Katie**    He loves you.

**Frank**    I love him.

**Katie**    He knows that.

**Frank**    I don't ever want to lose him.

**Katie**    You won't.

**Frank**    I don't ever want him to lose me.

**Frank** *begins to cry.*

I don't ever want him to come to any harm.

**Katie**    That's not possible.

**Frank**    I know.

**Katie** *comforts* **Frank**.

**Katie**    You can't protect him forever. You can only be there for him. Guide him. Give him the best possible start. You're trying. You're trying to make yourself a good role model. To bring him up in a civilised fashion. Unlike you. You were brought up in the madness. You're trying to break the chain. That's all you can do. Bubba can't pass on something he doesn't know. You're giving him good things to pass on. You're letting him know about them. You're planting a seed of civility. Gratitude. Humility. That will stand him in good stead. If things go tits up he'll always have that ingrained in his brain for him to fall back on. Hopefully it won't come to that but you can't control that you can only control what you pass on. You can only control who *you* are, not what *he* is. He's his own person. Let him live.

**Frank** *looks nonplussed*.

**Frank**    The way you let Chrissie live?

**Katie**    Touché.

**Katie** *laughs*.

**Frank**    Things would be better if there were more balance. Between us.

**Katie**    What do you mean?

**Frank**    If I were working.

**Katie**    He'll see you working. You got it in you.

**Frank**    Why do you stick with me?

**Katie**    Because I love you. Because I believe in you. Because I believe in the home I believe in family. Because I believe I'll reap the rewards. Because I'm co-dependent.

*They laugh.*

You're doing what you need to do. And it's working. It's got a long way to go yet mind . . .

*They laugh.*

But it's working.

**Frank**    Sometimes. I get all these good feelings inside me. Buzzing around. Swirling around and making me jumpy.

**Katie**    Why?

**Frank**    I worry someone's going to come along and take them.

**Katie**    Who?

**Frank**    Anyone.

**Katie**    Who?

**Frank** *thinks about it.*

You?

**Frank** *looks nonplussed.*

He believes in you why can't you?

**Frank**    What?

**Katie**    He chose you.

**Frank**    Who did?

**Katie**    He chose you to be his daddy. He took one look at you and he thought, yup, that's the guy I want, he'll do.

**Frank**    Is he mad?

**Katie**    I know.

**Frank**    Kid needs help.

**Katie** *laughs.*

**Katie**    I like it that you lied.

**Frank**    What?

**Katie**    About the boys. Next door. You don't have to impress me.

**Frank**    I wasn't impressing you.

**Katie**    Who were you impressing? Dee?

**Frank**    I was impressing you.

**Katie** *laughs.*

**Katie**    I like you as you are. Shit at video games.

**Frank** *gives a look and* **Katie** *laughs.*

Frank.

**Frank**    What?

**Katie**    If you do write again.

**Frank**    Yeah?

**Katie**    Don't forget about me.

**Frank**    What?

**Katie**    You heard.

**Frank**    As if.

**Katie**    I know what you're like.

**Frank**    I'm not like anything.

**Katie**   You heard.

**Frank** *looks nonplussed.*

**Frank**   Every word I write will be all about you.

**Katie**   Yeah right.

**Frank**   It's *true*.

**Katie**   Knowing you it'll be all about *you*.

**Frank**   It'll be all about them two.

*They laugh.*

**Katie**   Oi watch it you. I don't want to be falling out with the neighbours.

**Frank**   Come here.

**Frank** *grabs* **Katie** *and holds her in a clinch.*

Who's going to leave you you're beautiful.

**Katie**   Don't try and sweet-talk me.

**Frank**   I'm not. You're really beautiful. Put a bit of make-up on . . .

**Katie** *laughs.*

**Katie**   I'm going to bed I'm knackered.

**Frank**   Fine.

**Katie**   Is that alright?

**Frank**   I'll be right down.

**Katie**   Why don't you come down now?

**Frank**   What?

**Katie**   You heard.

**Frank**   I thought you were knackered?

**Katie**   I am.

**Frank** *looks nonplussed.*

**Frank**    Okay let's go down now.

**Katie**    Not before you clean up.

**Frank**    Of course not. Sorry I forgot myself there.

**Frank** *shakes his head.*

What was I thinking?

**Katie**    I need to phone Zane.

**Frank**    Oh yeah.

**Katie**    Turn the dishwasher on.

**Frank**    I will.

**Katie**    And the lights.

**Frank** *nods like he's heard the drill a thousand times.*

**Frank**    Katie.

**Katie**    What?

**Frank**    You really think everything happens for a reason?

**Katie**    Of course.

**Frank**    Why did Rich die?

**Katie**    What?

**Frank**    You heard.

**Katie**    I don't know.

**Frank** *nods.*

Why do I have to know?

**Frank**    I just thought you might.

**Katie**    Why do we have to know everything all the time?
Why can't we accept there are some things we don't know.

**Frank**    His wife and kids might want to know.

**Katie**   Maybe they will. In the fullness of time. Maybe not tomorrow maybe not in a thousand years. It's their story. There's a reason why bad things happen. Do you think your dad died in vain? Or is he benefiting Bubba in some way?

**Frank**   He's benefiting Bubba.

**Katie**   Of course he is. He did things you don't want to repeat. Things you saw with your own two eyes. You felt the consequences. Now you bring that to the table. It's in your armoury. You pick up your kid and you say we're taking that path, and he says why daddy and you say because I've seen what's down that path and I don't like it, it's no good, and he goes okay daddy. Well who showed you that path?

**Frank**   My old man.

**Katie**   He trod that path with you in tow and you fought your way back and now you know which path to take your boy.

**Frank**   That's exactly what I did. Followed dad. As a little boy I was always walking behind him. I was always imploring him not to do things. Things that would embarrass me. I used to wake up thinking what's he going to do today, but I never said that I just held tight and wished, wished that somehow my old man would come back again, the dad I used to know, I didn't realise how that was affecting me, I blocked off all emotion, I just sat tight and hoped the day would pass without too much going wrong, and when it did go wrong I didn't shout and wail and cry, I tried to make him better, I tried to make things better, I forgot that I was someone in all of this, I was a kid I didn't know any better I just found a way of living and I lived it, and that way was to lose touch with who I was, what was going on inside, I stopped expressing it, I just got through life as kids do, pretended nothing was happening when deep down a lot was happening I can see that now, I was angry, my whole world had fallen apart, I was sad, I'd lost my dad.

**Katie** *starts crying.*

Why are you crying?

**Katie**  Chrissie.

**Frank** *nods.*

**Frank**  It wasn't until *I* became a dad that I realised how much all this stuff means.

**Katie**  Or until you became clean.

**Frank** *looks nonplussed.*

**Frank**  Yeah.

**Frank** *nods.*

I'm going to make him proud of me.

**Katie**  Who?

**Frank**  What?

**Katie**  Your son or your dad?

**Frank** *looks nonplussed. His eyes well up.*

**Frank**  Go downstairs.

**Katie** *collects her mobile and walks off, going downstairs.* **Frank** *calls after her.*

Katie.

**Katie**  What?

**Frank**  Don't forget about me.

**Frank** *tidies up the kitchen, throwing the takeaway cartons and the tea bag in the bin, loading the plates, glasses, mug and cutlery in the dishwasher, putting a tablet in the dishwasher and turning it on, hanging the tea towel, cleaning the surfaces with the cloth, closing the cupboards, putting the ice tray in the freezer, putting the milk, apple juice and coke in the fridge. Finally he picks up the bottle of rum, looks at it, holds it upside down over the sink, waits for the last drop to spill, and puts it in the recycling. He flicks off the telly with the remote and turns off the lights, making the stage black.*

**The End**

Printed in the USA
CPSIA information can be obtained
at www.ICGtesting.com
LVHW020840171024
794056LV00002B/307